The First Sergeant

GETTING STARTED

Written by 1SG Jessie W. Sasser

Copyright

MADE IN AMERICA

Information herein was collected and composed by Jessie W. Sasser

Copyright © 2012 by FirstSergeant.com / Jessie W. Sasser

Published through Google electronically, also available in paperback

ISBN: **978-0-615-68390-4**

No part of this publication may be reproduced, stored in a retrieval system or transmitted in any form or by any means, electronic, mechanical, photocopying, recording, scanning or otherwise, except as permitted under Sections 107 or 108 of the 1976 United States Copyright Act, without either the prior written permission of the Publisher, or authorization through payment of the appropriate per-copy fee to the Copyright Clearance Center, 8002A Barstow Rd. Ft Irwin CA 92310, (910)916-0257 or online at http://www.FirstSergeant.com/ .

Limit of Liability / Disclaimer of Warranty: The Publisher and author make no representations or warranties with respect to the accuracy or completeness of the contents of this work and specifically disclaim all warranties, including without limitation warranties of fitness for a particular purpose. No warranty may be created or extended by sales or promotional materials. The advice and strategies contained herein may not be suitable for every situation. This work is sold with the understanding that the publisher is not engaged in rendering legal, accounting, or other professional services. If professional assistance is required, the services of a competent professional person should be sought. Neither the publisher nor the author shall be liable for damages arising here from. The fact that an organization or website is referred to in this work as a citation and or potential source of further information does not mean that the author or the publisher endorses the information the organization or website may provide or recommendations it may make. Further, readers should be aware that Internet Websites listed in this work may have changed or disappeared between when this work was written and when it is read. This book does not supplement doctrine.

Library of Congress Cataloging-in-Publication Data:

Library of Congress Control Number: **2012946996**

Library of Congress
US & Publisher Liaison Division
Cataloging in Publication Program
101 Independence Avenue, S.E.
Washington, DC 20540-4283

TRADEMARKS: www.FirstSergeant.com, FirstSergeant.com, and FirstSergeant are trademarks or registered trademarks of FirstSergeant.com and/or its affiliates, in the United States and other countries, and may not be used without written permission. All other trademarks are the property of their respective owners.

Table of Contents

Copyright 2
    Creed of the Noncommissioned Officer 9
Preface 10
Design Usage 11
Acknowledgments 11
Assuming Command 12
    Building Relationships 12
        1SG / Commander 12
        1SG / 1SG 13
        1SG / XO 13
        1SG / PSG 13
        1SG / PL 14
        1SG / OPS SGM 14
        1SG / CSM 14
        1SG / RSM / BDE CSM 15
        1SG / Soldiers 15
    Establishing OPS 16
        Alpha Roster 17
        Additional Alpha Roster Info 17
        Special Skills Tracker 18
        Additional Skills Tracker Info 18
        Rating Scheme 19
    Administration 19
        NCOERs 19
        Awards 20
        SSD (Structured Self Development) 20
        Military Schooling 21

- Tasking FRAGOs 21
- Troop to Task 22
- Duty Roster 22
- Training Schedule 23
- Battle Rhythm 24
- UCMJ 24

Leadership Theories 25
- Trait Theory 25
- Contingency Theory 26
- Situational Theory 26
- Behavioral Theory 26
- Participative Theory 26
- Management Theory 26
- Relationship Theory 27

Safety Brief 28
- If you drink "don't drive" / if you drive "don't drink" 28
- POV safety, wear seatbelts, don't speed, and don't drive sleepy 28
- Let me bail you out before you go to jail 28
- Don't do drugs / Stay away from spice and bath salt 28
- Keep the barracks clean / CDR can initiate H&W at any time 28
- Avoid domestic violence / walk away 29
- Suicide is a selfish act, look for indicators in others 29
- Safe Sex 29
- Motorcycle Safety / wear proper gear and stay alert 29
- Swimming / need lifeguard on duty / avoid unauthorized areas 29
- Weapon Safety / keep guns in arms room / and be safe hunting 29
- Keep up the good work – stay motivated 29

Sexual Assault Prevention and Response Program 30
- Policy, DoD Guidance, Regulations, and Memorandums 30
- The goals of the Sexual Assault Prevention and Response Program are: 30
- Reporting options: Restricted / Unrestricted Reporting 30

Understanding DoD's Confidentiality Policy 31
Restricted Reporting 31
Who may make a Restricted Report 32
Restricted Reporting example 33
Considerations when electing a Restricted Reporting decision 34
Benefits 34
Limitations 34
Unrestricted Reporting 35
Unrestricted Reporting example 35
SHARP Conclusion 36

Training 37
Introduction 37
Mandatory Training in Units 37
Preparation for Training 39
Training Models 40
The Eight-Step Training Model 40
Example Training Story Board 42

Responsibilities 43
Overview 43
Purpose 43
Scope 43
General 43
Teamwork 43
Commander's Intent 44
Conditions set by the 1SG 44
Competence 44
Physical Fitness & Military Bearing 44
Leading 45
Training 46
Responsibility & Accountability 46
Administration 47

- Discipline 48
  - Indicators of Poor Leadership 48
  - Indicators of Outstanding Leadership 49
  - Zero Tolerance Items 49
  - 100% Your Responsibility 49
- Counseling Formats 50
  - Lower enlisted initial 50
    - Possible Key Points for Discussion: 50
    - Attitude 50
    - AWOL Prevention 50
    - Barracks Life Rules 50
    - Command Maintenance 51
    - Chaplain 51
    - Complaint Procedures 51
    - Crime Prevention 51
    - Family Care Plans 51
    - Dining Facility Dress 52
    - Driving under the Influence / Abuse Prevention and Control 52
    - Equal Opportunity 52
    - Leave/Pass 52
    - Physical Fitness 53
    - Privately Owned Weapons (POWs) 53
    - Redress of Grievances 53
    - Reenlistment Incentives 53
    - Safety 53
    - Separate Rations 54
    - Sexual Harassment 54
    - Sick Call Procedures 54
    - Suicide Prevention 54
    - Possible Plan of Action: 54
  - Indebtedness 55

Plan of Action: 55
DUI 56
    Possible Key Points for Discussion: 56
    Possible Plan of Action: 56
Overweight 57
    Possible Key Points for Discussion: 57
    Possible Plan of Action: 57
Pregnancy 58
    Possible Key Points for Discussion: 58
    Possible Plan of Action: 59
Family Care Plan 59
    Possible Key Points for Discussion: 59
    Possible Plan of Action: 60
Promotion 61
    Possible Key Points for Discussion: 61
    Possible Plan of Action: 61
Motorcycle Ownership 62
    Possible Key Points for Discussion: 62
    Possible Plan of Action: 62
WLC 63
    Possible Key Points for Discussion: 63
    Possible Plan of Action: 64
SSD 65
    Possible Key Points for Discussion: 65
    Possible Plan of Action: 66
Counseling Disciplinary Clause 66
    Legal statement version #1 66
    Legal statement version #2 66
    Legal statement version #3 67
Counseling Examples 68
    AWOL 68

Drug Related Incident 69
Marijuana 70
Cocaine 70
Ecstasy and Amphetamine 71
Lost ID Card 72
Jump Refusal 72
Speeding 73
Jump Master Proficiency 74
Insubordination 75
Extra Duty and Restriction 76
Example Memorandum 78
Flow Charts 79
    4833 Processing 80
    UCFR 81
    Monthly Hand Receipt 82
    Sensitive Items Inventory 83
    PAI Procedures 84
    GPC Card 85
    Urinalysis 85
    Schools 87
    Counseling 87
    AWOL 89
    DFR 90
    AWOL / DFR INV 91
    Suicide Ideation / Attempt 92
    Positive UA 93
    DUI 94
    Domestic Abuse 95
    Lautenberg Amendment 96
    Sexual Harassment 97
    Sexual Assault 98

WTB Nomination 99
Hospitalization 100
Family Care Plan 101
Suspense of Favorable Actions 102
Bar to Reenlistment 103
FLIPL 104
Soldier Death 105
EFMP 106
Health and Welfare Inspections 107
Off Post Apprehension / Confinement 108
Advancement Wavers 109

Reference Information 110
  Reference Manuals 110
  MIRANDA RIGHTS WARNING STATEMENT 111
  Punitive articles UCMJ 112
    Article 134-General article 113
  Acronyms 115

About the Author 121

Creed of the Noncommissioned Officer

No one is more professional than I. I am a Noncommissioned Officer, a leader of soldiers. As a noncommissioned officer, I realize that I am a member of a time honored corps, which is known as "the Backbone of the Army." I am proud of the Corps of Noncommissioned Officers and will at all times conduct myself so as to bring credit upon the Corps, the military service and my country regardless of the situation in which I find myself. I will not use my grade or position to attain pleasure, profit or personal safety.

Competence is my watch-word. My two basic responsibilities will always be uppermost in my mind – accomplishment of my mission and the welfare of my soldiers. I will strive to remain technically and tactically proficient. I am aware of my role as a noncommissioned officer. I will fulfill my responsibilities inherent in that role. All soldiers are entitled to outstanding leadership; I will provide that leadership. I know my soldiers and I will always place their needs above my own. I will communicate consistently with my soldiers and never leave them uninformed. I will be fair and impartial when recommending both rewards and punishment.

Officers of my unit will have maximum time to accomplish their duties; they will not have to accomplish mine. I will earn their respect and confidence as well as that of my soldiers. I will be loyal to those with whom I serve; seniors, peers and subordinates alike. I will exercise initiative by taking appropriate action in the absence of orders. I will not compromise my integrity, nor my moral courage. I will not forget, nor will I allow my comrades to forget that we are professionals, Noncommissioned Officers, leaders!

Preface

What makes a great leader? I would say experience, knowledge, and the desire to lead. Throughout my profession, I have been fortunate enough to work with such great leaders. There was a point in my military career years ago when I was required to wear civilian clothes to work and knew people only by their first name. This was a very exciting time in my life but there was one moment that stands out above the rest. I was new to the Unit so I did not know everyone or exactly how things operated. I was sitting in a conference room filled with people waiting to receive a mission brief. Several people were coming and going when a man walked in and stated, "Let's get started". The thing about this person is I had no idea who he was, but after ten minutes, I was ready to follow him into battle without a doubt. It didn't matter if he out ranked me, hell he could have been a civilian for all I knew but he was a true leader, ready to lead and answer any question you had.

First Sergeants lead by example. Much like the man in my story, they have to be that person who walks in the room and gains respect through their words and actions not just from the diamond they wear on their chest. It's being an unqualified expert in promotions, demotions, billeting, marksmanship, counseling, evaluations, inspections, public speaking, leave & passes, medical benefits, military law, civilian law, military aid, child and family support, unit history, parades, ceremonies, family advocacy, standards and discipline, UCMJ, reenlistment, retirement, weight control, professional military education, ID card privileges, off limits areas, restrictions, and so on... Its selfless service at its finest, carrying a cell phone 24 hours a day 7 days a week not complaining when they get a call at 0200hrs on a Sunday morning to bail a Soldier out of jail, then another call at 0600hrs to settle a domestic dispute. We deal with situations like true professionals putting our emotions aside in order to create an environment that fosters those same Army values that made us who we are.

We do not do things because we are bored; we do things because we are always moving forward. Sometimes we seek out personal ventures like writing this book for instance and sometimes we dedicate our time completely to our Soldiers. As a First Sergeant, you should strive to keep that momentum going. Try not to spend more than 24 months in a command. Six years as a First Sergeant in the same company might not look as good as a First Sergeant that had three different positions gaining experience from each. There is a saying that the further you are from the flag pole the more likely you are to drift in discipline. This is the same for time in position. Make it known that you are ready and willing to accept new challenges.

Design Usage

This book is designed to be very practical. It will give you a brief overview and quick insight on some of the most critical topics First Sergeants and other senior leaders deal with on a daily bases, intended for new First Sergeants and Platoon Sergeants aspiring to take that next step. I have included flow charts to help provide additional guidance when faced with certain complex situations. For a more elaborate discussion or detailed description on each topic refer to military doctrine or visit www.FirstSergeant.com . There you will find several example files used throughout this book.

Acknowledgments

I would like to thank the following for their support, input and or recommendations, without them, this book would not be possible.

Extremely competent professionals in alphabetical order:

Clauer, Michael F. CPT USA

Gregory, Charles W. CSM USA

Martin, Thomas O. 1LT USA

Pinkney, Lewis 1SG USA

Reed, Kurt L. CSM USA

Assuming Command

Building Relationships

1SG / Commander

I suggest that during the first week you sit down with your Commander and guarantee your commitment to service and duty. Reassure them that you are there to enforce their standards and that you will do your best to understand their intentions. This conversation should last about two hours. Take the initiative to go to them first and keep this separate from your initial counseling. This will allow for a more open-ended conversation. Other topics for discussion should include family, hobbies, experiences, where you are from, and of course the future of your company. You should also establish the "zero tolerance" list, covered later in the topic **Conditions set by the 1SG**. With these standards determined up front, there should be little question as to what warrants UCMJ. Going to your Commander before he/she comes to you shows confidence and discussing these topics shows experience. This is the initial phase of trust building that will eventually be critical when it comes to saving your Commander's career. Try to establish a truly mutual relationship. The minute your Commander has to order you to do something verses requesting it, a certain respect has been lost by both parties that can be very hard to recover.

Chances are you probably have more stripes then they have years in service. Your goal is to convince them they would do well to draw on your counsel at times. Ensure they have the tools to be successful. If it looks like they are getting ready to slip-up, do your job and advise them. It is imperative that you and your Commander have a great working relationship, and if you do not, it needs to look that way. One voice. Never talk them down to others, and be prepared to explain their mistakes. If there are major, evident problems just remember that you are working through it and with your experience and knowledge; everything should be back on track soon.

"Commanders and First Sergeants are not friends. Their relationship is more important than that. It is a bond based on mutual trust and respect- a bond that exists from the moment the battalion Commander passes the guidon to the Company Commander. The First Sergeant does not think, "You, Company Commander, have to earn my respect"- that respect is automatically given to the

Commander. The Army cannot afford the time for respect to be built- the unit may have to go to combat the next day. This mutual respect is based on understanding the backgrounds of the two individuals, and their mutual dedication to the service of their country. As the Company Commander and First Sergeant work together, this bond can be strengthened, weakened, or broken. A weakened relationship can be repaired through honest dialogue. But once broken, this bond cannot be restored. The command team must know each other's strengths and weaknesses, because those are the team's strengths and weaknesses. For the command team to reach a point of tangency, it must use the strengths to its greatest advantage while covering for the other's weaknesses even if it means breaking with traditional officer/NCO roles." - CSM Jimmie W. Spencer, letter 1 Sep 1997

1SG / 1SG

You should be replacing a First Sergeant or an acting First Sergeant, they will be able to provide valuable background information on any Soldier's issues and the unit's strengths and weaknesses. Ask for any product they may have saved, it could keep you from reinventing the wheel. During your transition take advantage of their time, and make sure you get their e-mail address. This will prove helpful in the event there is a dispute dealing with decisions they have made in the past.

1SG / XO

Your XO should respect your decisions and turn to you for guidance. In order to establish this professional relationship you need to understand the role and responsibilities of the executive officer. Together you are responsible for the "Beans and Bullets". Generally, executive officers handle equipment movement while 1SGs handle Troop to Task and personnel movement, therefore communication between you is extremely critical. Groom this person into an outstanding Soldier that always upholds standards and respects NCOs, they will be a Company Commander soon.

1SG / PSG

Your platoon sergeants are your direct link to your Soldiers. Your platoon sergeants work for you, so you must demand respect and loyalty. Make them understand that they do not talk about each other and encourage positive feedback. It fosters an environment that your NCOs will want to be a part of. Promote Esprit de Corps and an environment that will help them understand your company is a team and the competition is other units. Your goal is to blur the line between platoons when it comes to accomplishing the mission utilizing teamwork but to instigate competitiveness when it comes to standards. If for some reason you have a platoon sergeant that refuses to be a team player or constantly violates your trust, it will create a toxic work environment and therefore should be resolved at the lowest level. Negative counseling statements given to your PSGs by you should be brought to your CSM's attention. If it is a matter of personality conflict or the NCO has become a leadership challenge that you just cannot overcome, the issue might be resolved through a transfer of the NCO. If all else fails, you can request a Relief for Cause. Your paperwork must be in order if you intend on pursuing this option.

1SG / PL

Stick with professional guidance that will keep them out of trouble. You are one of the most experienced Soldiers in your company. Based on your experience and personal qualities, you should proactively mentor your Lieutenants in all aspects of professionalism, discipline, personnel management, maintenance, tactics or any other subject as appropriate. You are never to have an overt confrontation with a Lieutenant; you are a team and should resolve all issues behind closed doors when required. Rely on your maturity, experience, and professionalism to ensure this is consistently accomplished.

1SG / OPS SGM

This is most likely your next position and your direct link to S-3 plans. It is a thankless job so be patient and understanding when you are tasked with memorandums, labor, or duties with little to no notice. In most cases these tasks are not just produced by the SGM, it is more likely a directive from the S-3 or higher.

1SG / CSM

Respect the CSM because everyone needs guidance at some point, as a First Sergeant you are not an exception to that philosophy. The CSM has held your position and has walked in your shoes; he knows all too well the stressors involved in managing Soldiers and their problems. Every leader has their own leadership style, if there is a personality conflict or for some reason you have a disagreement, address the issues tactfully and make every effort to resolve your differences. All Soldiers, BN, BDE, and even Division leadership in some cases notice this relationship. The CSM that had a very successful assignment generally had a squared away 1SG team to support him.

1SG / RSM / BDE CSM

In most cases, the BDE CSM assigned you as First Sergeant so respect them for the opportunity they have given you. You would be lucky to make this level of responsibility in your career. This is a true Soldier full of experience that has been hardened through time, deserving of the utmost respect. Do your best to be professional in their presence and, short of greeting them, do not to interject your opinion unless you have something intelligent to say.

1SG / Soldiers

My favorite subject, Soldiers. Take care of your Soldiers, be hard but fair and do not ever lie to them. They will see through your bullshit and lose all respect for you. Be compassionate and show understanding but know when to draw the line. Just like any businessperson, a Soldier will take advantage of you if they can. Soldiers will come to you to solve their problems, so it is imperative that you have a good understanding of all support services the military has to offer. Remember, your primary responsibility lies with your Soldiers. This is easily forgotten when dealing with an irate spouse or creditor, especially when you know your Soldier is at fault. Do not be so quick to judge them; after all, you were young once. You should advise your Soldier on how to recover from the situation, not the spouse or creditor on how they can make it worse. Make your Soldiers uphold the standards through discipline and commendation, they will respect you for it. When they excel recognize them with reward and compensation, it shows how much you appreciate them.

"They obey orders instantly and without hesitation, but they are not without spirit or individual dignity. They are self-sufficient. They have two sets of fatigues: they wash one and wear the other. They keep their canteens full and their feet dry. They sometimes forget to brush their teeth, but never to clean their rifle. They can cook their own meals, mend their own clothes, and fix their own hurts. If you are thirsty, they will share their water with you, if you are hungry, their food. They will even split their ammunition with you in the midst of battle when you run low.

They have learned to use their hands like weapons and weapons as if they were their hands. They can save your life – or take it, because that is their job. They will often do twice the work of a civilian, draw half the pay and still find ironic humor in it all. They have seen more suffering and death then they should have in their career. Take care of your Soldiers."

Establishing OPS

Assuming no one handed you a continuity book full of answers, you will need to establish one. Also referred to as your *Leader's Book,* still required in some units. However, with advancement in technology and increased use of digital media it has become the norm to have everything in your phone, tablet or stored on your laptop. You WILL need working knowledge of computers and file management. If you have problems operating a mouse, I suggest you learn. This is a weakness among some senior NCOs, however, most have adapted. Establishing a good working OPS means, you need a good OPS NCO. Do not settle for a substandard Soldier. Most Unit Manning Reports (UMRs) do not account for an Operations NCO so I suggest holding mandatory interviews for the position. If you get a squared away NCO, they can also hold the position as Headquarters Platoon Sergeant.

Your digital leader's book should be well organized and kept in the My Documents folder. Expect to access these folders and files often, several times a day. You will receive Request for Information (RFIs) that on most occasions require an immediate response. I will cover some critical documents that I have personally found necessary in order to be successful.

Make note of the .pst file in *Figure 1 [Example Documents Folders]* this file is a backup of all your e-mails from Microsoft Outlook. You should create a .pst file and maintain a copy for future reference.

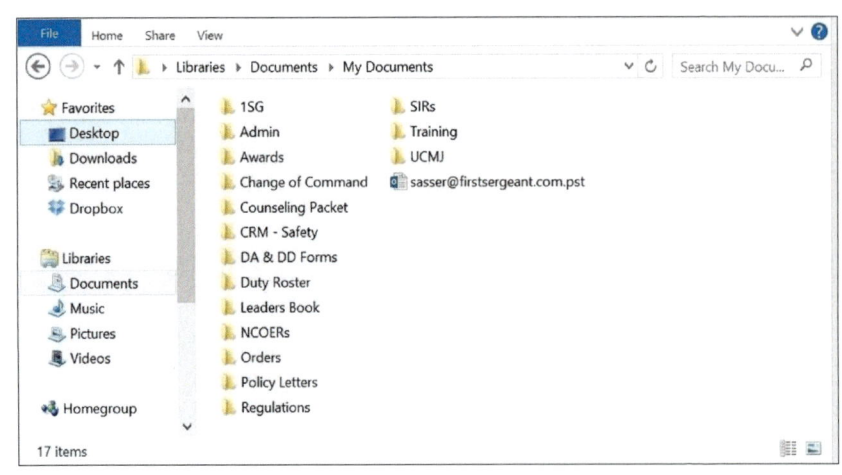

Figure 1 [Example Documents Folders]

HWAC

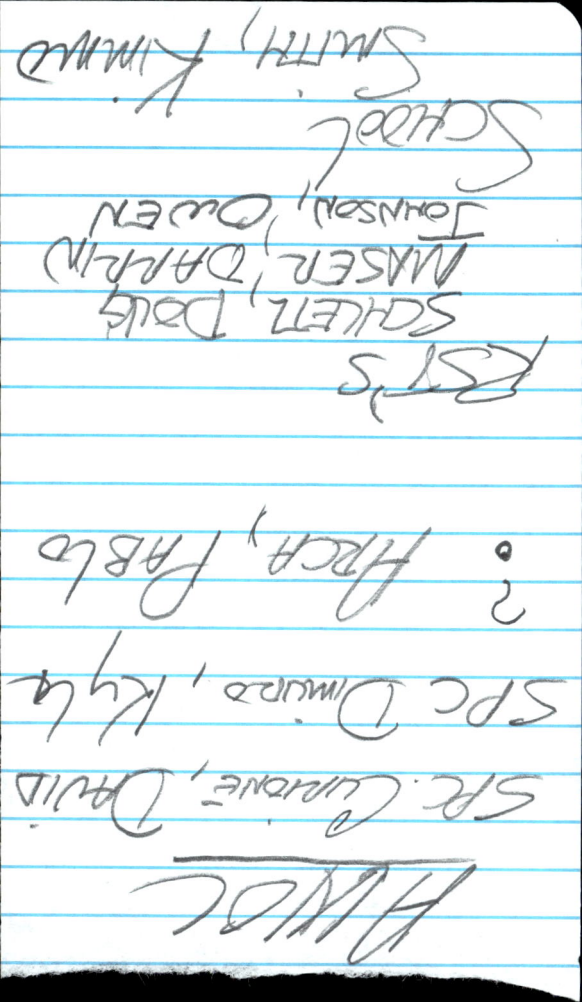

SPC Cimone, David

SPC Dimitro, Kyle

? Hirth, Parker

RST's
Schlett, Doug
Maser, Dahlin
Johnson, Owen

School
Smith, Kimmie

Alpha Roster

The Alpha roster contains sensitive information about every Soldier assigned to your unit. Handle this document with extreme care and take every precaution to keep this information safe and out of the wrong hands. You may wish to add additional information based on your requirement. This document along with other examples were created using Microsoft Office. Generally, MS Office comes preinstalled on government computers but there is a free version that will open and edit the same file types called Open Office. In addition, Microsoft offers an inexpensive version of Office if you are military through the Home Use Program.

Combine your data into one document either by putting all info on the same spreadsheet (which would be very large and impractical) or by adding tabs to the bottom for the different types of information. Here is a list of additional information that might appear. Collect this information on the Soldier's Personal Data Sheet during in processing with a hardcopy stored in their file folder and Counseling Packet.

Format: Microsoft Excel
Produced by: Company
Composed and Maintained by: OPS NCO
Figure 2 [Example Alpha Roster]

	A	B	C	D	E	F	G
1	RANK	LAST	FIRST	MI	SSN	MOS	BLOOD
2	PVT	AWESOME	JOE	L	987-76-5432	19D	OPOS
3	PFC	BEST	JIM	W	555-44-3333	91B	ABPOS
4	PVT	COOL	JESSE	R	444-55-3333	31L	ONEG
5	SPC	DETERMINED	JONES	J	999-66-2311	88M	BPOS
6							
7							

Additional Alpha Roster Info

- Address
- Date of birth
- Age
- Weight
- Height
- Hair color
- Eye color
- DOR
- BASD
- ETS
- TIG

- TIS
- Religion
- Phone Number
- Marital status
- Spouse's name
- Children's name
- Next of Kin
- APFT
- Equipment sizes
- POV information

Special Skills Tracker

The Special Skills Tracker is a great source of information when kept updated. Generally, it will cover your requirements for qualified personnel and show what you actually have on hand. Need to know how many bus drivers you have or who are licensed? This is where you find it. The OPS SGM normally maintains it at the BN / SQDN level but I suggest keeping a copy on your computer. Files get corrupt or deleted and a lot of effort goes into having an accurate skills tracker. Below you will find additional skills that may have administrative value.

Format: Microsoft Excel
Produced by: BN / SQDN
Composed and Maintained by: 1SG / OPS NCO / OPS SGM

Figure 3 [Example Special Skills Tracker]

	A	B	C	D	E	F	G	H	I	J	K	L	M	N
1	Position	Required	HHC			A CO			B CO			C CO		
2			Req	O/H	Slots Reqd	Req	O/H	Slots Reqd	Req	O/H	Slots Reqd	Req	O/H	Slots Reqd
3	Jump Master	1 per 10 Jumpers	14	0	0	8	7	1	8	0	8	8	0	8
4	DZSO	All Jump Masters	14	0	14	8	0	8	8	0	8	8	0	8
5	Assistant DZSO	2 per PLT	8	0	8	8	0	8	8	0	8	6	0	6
6	DACO	1 per PLT	4	0	4	4	0	4	4	0	4	3	0	3
7	RANGER		0	14	-14	3	5	-2	3	1	1	2	6	-4
8	RSLC	All 11 Series & 19D MOS	0	0	0	0	8	-8	0	0	0	0	23	0
9	Sniper	All assigned M24	0	0	0	0	1	-1	0	0	0	7	6	1
10	Pathfinder		0	3	-3	0	2	-2	0	0	0	18	0	18
11	EIB	ALL 11A/11B/11C		8	-8		3	-3		3	3		29	-29
12	EIA				0		3	-3			0		0	0
13	Combatives	Level I / 1 Inst. Per PLT	3	0	3	4	6	0	4	0	4	3	1	2
14		Level II/ 1 Inst. Per TRP	1	1	0	1	5	-4	1	2	-1	1	0	1
15		Level III / 1 Inst. Per SQDN	0	0	0	0	1	-1	0	0	0	0	0	0
		Level IV / 1 Inst.												

Tabs: Master | Jump Master | Sniper | Bus Driver | Range Control | ENV COMPLIANCE | Combatives LV 1 | Combatives LV 2 | Combatives LV 3

Additional Skills Tracker Info

Jump Master	CPOF	COIST	HAZMAT	WLC
DZSO	Armorer	OPSEC	UMO	ALC PH 1
Assistant DZSO	BATTLE STAFF	ETRP/ECA	AMO	ALC PH2
DACO	JAVELIN	IED Defeat	AALPS	SLC
NAPs	PMCS LDR's Course	Tactical IO	TMDE Coord	Mail Handler
RANGER	RAVEN	C-IED	USE Cert	DTMS
RSLC	CAO/CNO	EFMB	TC-AIMS II	DTS
Sniper	CLEAR	CLS	PBUSE	UARS
Pathfinder	Safety Officer	EMT	SAMS-E	Range Control
EIB	Bus Driver	Master Res Tng	ENVIR Comp	AMMO Handler
EIA	EOR	ATLS	Customs Trained	Master Gunner
Combatives	UPL	SHARP	JFC	Master Driver
IMLC	Field Sanitation	DIV PCC	JFO	Tactical Air Ops

Rating Scheme

Another roster or tracker that should be maintained at your level and constantly monitored is your company rating scheme. You have to stay on top of this! Not only should you coordinate the timeliness in which the forms are turned in, but also in most cases, you are the final person to verify the form is accurate and filled out correctly. You need a roster telling you when NCOERs are due and who is writing them. This tracker may be produced by higher or at company level, generally it is normally verified by the CSM and maintained at BN / SQDN level then briefed during your Command and Staff.

Format: Microsoft Excel
Produced by: Company / BN / SQDN
Composed and Maintained by: 1SG / OPS NCO / CSM / S1
Figure 4[Example Rating Scheme]

	A	B	C	D	E	F	G
1	RANK	LAST	DOR	SSN	MOS	THRU DATE	RATER
2	SGT	AWESOME	8/4/2012	987-76-5432	19D	8/4/2013	SSG MAD
3	SGT	BEST	9/9/2011	555-44-3333	91B	9/3/2013	SSG CRAZY
4	SSG	COOL	1/3/2010	444-55-3333	31L	12/4/2013	SFC INDEF
5	SFC	DETERMINED	3/1/2009	999-66-2311	88M	2/2/2014	1LT LOST

Administration

NCOERs

You, your NCOs, and officers must understand NCOERs. The best way to accomplish this is through LPD. We have created a two-page tool that will assist in establishing formatting standards. During Leaders Professional Development (LPD) explain the process used for correcting NCOERs then give them the tool with an uncorrected NCOER. They have 20 minutes to make corrections. You can find this example free at the following website.

http://www.firstsergeant.com/

NCOER forms change often so stay updated on the latest version. Ref. DA PAM 623-3 and AR 623-3. NCOERs are nothing new for senior NCOs, but as the First Sergeant, you have to have advanced knowledge on formatting and content. You are responsible for reviewing and correcting every NCOER submitted by your company.

Format: Forms Viewer DA Form 2166-8
Produced by: Company
Composed and Maintained by: Rater / Reviewed by 1SG

Awards

Awards can be very tricky, get with your S-1 and get an example AAM, ARCOM, and MSM. You should be tracking all ETS / PCS dates and have a draft award written 90 days out to account for corrections. Some units require submission to S-1 based on the type of award. Ensure retiring Soldiers receive an award that corresponds with their quality of service over the past 10 years; they will not be permitted to participate in the retirement ceremony without an award. Also, ensure PCSing Soldiers are suitably rewarded for their service. Get them in early, and remember that the stated award lead times are the minimum.

Format: Forms Viewer DA Form 638
Produced by: Recommender
Composed and Maintained by: Recommender / 1SG

SSD (Structured Self Development)

SSD is the latest in professional military education, now a requirement for advancement in the Army. The intent of SSD is to bridge the operational and institutional domains and set conditions for continuous growth. SSD will ensure learning is continuous and enduring, not sporadic and transitory. SSD is required learning that continues throughout a career and is closely linked to and synchronized with classroom and experiential learning. SSD is both an individual and first line leader responsibility executed at the individual's pace but under the supervision of the first line leader. SSD is a centrally managed set of specified content that you must complete within specified career points as a prerequisite for attendance at warrior, senior leader, and SGM courses. SSD is a prerequisite for attendance to NCOES courses effective 1 Oct 12.

As the First Sergeant, you have to ensure your Soldiers have the allotted time to accomplish this training. Soldiers can be counseled on SSD, see *SSD Example Counseling* in the back of this book. If a Soldier fails to show progress the Soldier can be administratively reduced or BARRED from reenlistment IAW AR 600-8-19, Chapter 10, para 10-5. The key is accurate counseling with follow-up assessments.

Format: ALMS through AKO
Produced by: Individual

Military Schooling

As with SSD your Soldiers can be administratively reduced or BARRED from reenlistment if they fail to show progress IAW AR 600-8-19, Chapter 10, para 10-5. A deliberate failure to attend WLC or ALC could serve as proof that the Soldier in question is unfit to serve in the grade of E-5 or E-6. For most schools there is a checklist with the First Sergeant's signature block verifying APFT, H/W, OCIE or any other prerequisites. Most schools requiring TDY will have an authorized use of the Government Travel Card in the orders. If your Soldier requires a Government Travel Card, get the paperwork submitted in advance IAW finance SOP. Counsel your Soldiers on this added responsibility. Maintain a company level OML for schools and waivers for promotion

Tasking FRAGOs

Another thing you should completely understand is taskings. From the moment, you take command you are given orders from higher, orders in the form of Daily Tasking FRAGOs (DTF), Weekly Tasking FRAGOs (WTF) and published Orders. I suggest you keep a digital copy of all published orders. Anything received in an e-mail should be saved in a folder and printed. You should go through and read every page highlighting anything pertaining to your company. Look for suspense dates and take note of them. The tasking and suspense date should then be discussed in your Platoon Sergeant meetings. Sometimes your battalion or squadron OPS SGM will publish a daily or weekly Task Tracker. If so, this will make things a little easier to keep track of. This tracker is normally produced by higher.

Format: Microsoft Excel
Produced by: BN / SQDN
Composed and Maintained by: OPS SGM
Figure 5[Example Task Tracker]

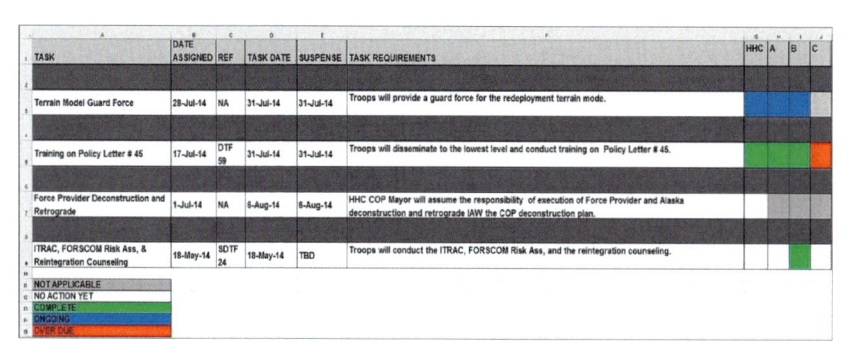

TASK	DATE ASSIGNED	REF	TASK DATE	SUSPENSE	TASK REQUIREMENTS	HHC	A	B	C
Terrain Model Guard Force	28-Jul-14	NA	31-Jul-14	31-Jul-14	Troops will provide a guard force for the redeployment terrain mode.				
Training on Policy Letter # 45	17-Jul-14	DTF 59	31-Jul-14	31-Jul-14	Troops will disseminate to the lowest level and conduct training on Policy Letter # 45.				
Force Provider Deconstruction and Retrograde	1-Jul-14	NA	6-Aug-14	6-Aug-14	HHC COP Mayor will assume the responsibility of execution of Force Provider and Alaska deconstruction and retrograde IAW the COP deconstruction plan.				
ITRAC, FORSCOM Risk Ass, & Reintegration Counseling	18-May-14	SDTF 24	18-May-14	TBD	Troops will conduct the ITRAC, FORSCOM Risk Ass, and the reintegration counseling.				

- NOT APPLICABLE
- NO ACTION YET
- COMPLETE
- ONGOING
- OVER DUE

Troop to Task

In addition to tracking tasks from higher, you will need to verify you have the manpower to accomplish the task. This is where you have to maintain a solid Troop-to-Task tracker. I normally had my PSGs update the OPS NCO every Friday for the following week. This is a good way of knowing what every Soldier is doing every day. Remember to trust but verify. Try to pull yourself away from the desk and check on your Soldiers periodically, it shows you have an interest in what they are doing and affords you the opportunity to verify the Troop-to-Task.

Format: Microsoft Excel
Produced by: Company
Composed and Maintained by: OPS NCO
Figure 6[Example Troop-to-Task]

	A	B	C	D	E	F	G	H	I
1	WEEK 15								
2	RANK	LAST	Monday	Tuesday	Wednesday	Thursday	Friday	Saturday	Sunday
3	SGT	HARD	OPS	OPS	MWR	OPS	ECP	OPS	OPS
4	SGT	DRIVER	SHARANA	SHARANA	GIRO	GIRO	SHARANA	SHARANA	SHARANA
5	SGT	SHARP	MISSION	MISSION	MISSION	MISSION	RECOVERY/RTO	MISSION PREP	MISSION
6	SPC	CLEANCUT	MISSION	MISSION	MISSION	MISSION	MWR	MISSION PREP	MISSION
7	PV2	POLICECALL	OPS	KP	OPS	ECP	ECP	CSM DETAIL	OPS
8	SPC	DIRECT				COOK			

Duty Roster

Your company will be responsible for providing Soldiers for Staff Duty. Most companies do not run a CQ anymore because of a reduction in force across the Army. However, if you are running a company level duty roster, ensure you deconflict it with other duties and that it reflects accurately on the troop-to-task. When establishing your DA 6 make sure it is in alphabetical order, this will save you an IG complaint. You are not always going to be able to keep the order and will have to replace Soldiers on duty. Minimize this as much as possible and, if required have the Soldiers directly swap dates, it will save you a lot of paperwork. You will notice this roster includes weekend duties, just ensure Soldiers are not pulling duty back to back.

Format: Forms Viewer / DA 6
Produced by: Company
Composed and Maintained by: 1SG
Figure 7[Example Duty Roster]

DUTY ROSTER		NATURE OF DUTY REOCCURRING										ORGANIZATION BEST UNIT IN THE WORLD									
GRADE	NAME	Month	AUGUST																		
		Day	1	2	3	4	5	6	7	8	9	10	11	12	13	14	15	16	17	18	19	20	21
E-2	AWESOME		X				X			X					X				X		
E-4	BEST			X				X		X	X					X			X			
E-4	COOL				X		X					X					X			X	X	
E-3	DETERMINED				X	X		X					X			X					X

Training Schedule

This schedule informs your Soldiers what is happening all day every day. This document should be posted for all Soldiers to see and should project out 4 – 8 weeks. The Company Commander normally produces and maintains this document with your input based on taskings and or training requirements. You establish the training requirements based on your company's Mission Essential Task List (METL). This can also be produced in calendar format.

Format: Microsoft Word / Microsoft Power Point
Produced by: Company
Composed and Maintained by: CDR

Figure 8[Example Training Schedule]

Best Unit in the World
Training Schedule for Period: 1/ Fiscal Year: 2014

Date	Start Time	End Time	Audience	Description/Notes	Instructor / Alternate	Uniform	Location	Reference
Feb 7, 2014	0630	0730	All	Physical Training	Platoon SGT's	APFU	COFF	TC 3-22.20
	0730	0900	All	Personal Hygiene/ Breakfast	Squad Leaders	MCU	TRP AO	FM 21-100/ 21 Day Master Menu
	0900	1200	All	Receive SI Container	2LT	MCU	TRP AO	FM 4-01
	1200	1300	All	Lunch	SFC	MCU	DFAC	21 Day Master Menu
	1300	1730	All(-)	Prep Weapons for SARET turn-in	SPC	MCU	TRP AO	Appropriate TMs
	1730	1800	All	Close Out Formation	1SG	MCU	COFF	FM 6-22

Figure 9[Example Training Calendar]

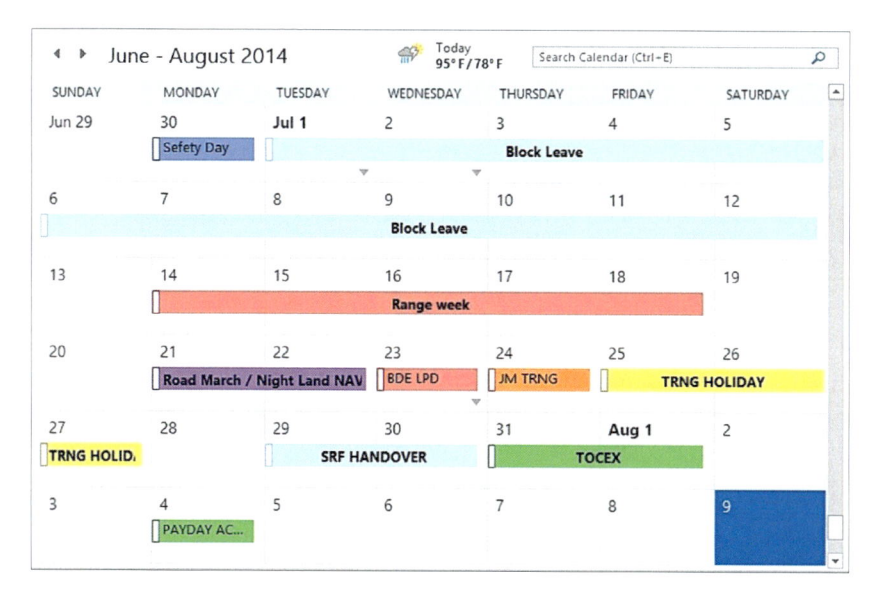

June - August 2014 — Today 95°F / 78°F

SUNDAY	MONDAY	TUESDAY	WEDNESDAY	THURSDAY	FRIDAY	SATURDAY
Jun 29	30 Safety Day	Jul 1	2	3 Block Leave	4	5
6	7	8	9 Block Leave	10	11	12
13	14	15	16 Range week	17	18	19
20	21 Road March / Night Land NAV	22	23 BDE LPD	24 JM TRNG	25 TRNG HOLIDAY	26
27 TRNG HOLID.	28	29	30 SRF HANDOVER	31	Aug 1 TOCEX	2
3	4 PAYDAY AC...	5	6	7	8	9

Battle Rhythm

Within the first week, you should also establish or adopt a good weekly battle rhythm. Determine key events that happen on a weekly basis and add it to your calendar. Microsoft Office has preset tools for this. This is not the training calendar so only put reoccurring events here. Post this in the CP.

Format: Microsoft Word / Microsoft Power Point
Produced by: Company
Composed and Maintained by: OPS NCO
Figure 10 [Example Battle Rhythm]

SUNDAY	MONDAY	TUESDAY	WEDNESDAY	THURSDAY	FRIDAY	SATURDAY
Jun 29	30 – 0900 S3 SY.	Jul 1	2 – 0900 CSM	3	4 – BUB	5
6	7 – 0900 S3 SY.	8 – 1000 G3 SY.	9 – 0900 CSM	10 – SGT TIM TR.	11 – WLC INBRIEF	12
13	14 – 0900 S3 SY.	15	16 – 0900 CSM	17	18 – BUB	19
20	21 – 0900 S3 SY.	22	23 – 0900 CSM	24 – SGT TIME T..	25	26
27	28 – 0900 S3 SY.	29	30	31	Aug 1 – BUB	2
3	4	5	6	7 – SGT TIME T..	8	9

UCMJ

Another topic you will deal with is UCMJ. You should review all recommendations for UCMJ with the entire counseling packet for validation, looking for possible patterns of misconduct or failed rehabilitation. In some cases, you will be the one recommending the Soldier for UCMJ. Ensure the negative counseling has the legal statement, for examples see **Legal Statements** in the back of this book.

You start by gathering the actual counseling's for recommendation and any sworn statements necessary. Once satisfied the negative behavior merits discipline, flag the Soldier for adverse action. Bring these documents to your legal representative for processing. Within 72 hours, your legal rep should have built a proceedings packet. Normally when you open the packet, you will see all possible punishment on the left with adverse actions and proceedings on the right. You or your commander should read the initial portion on the proceeding side to the Soldier, than they have 72 hours to see Trial Defense Services (TDS). Finally, your commander will bring the Soldier in for their final reading. The Soldier should have the opportunity to plead their case providing any paperwork or witnesses pertaining to the allegations. Tell the Soldier to standby outside the room during deliberation. The commander should take input from the leadership and your recommendation. Remember, zero tolerance means there are NO excuses for violations. Things are not always black and white; consider everything when making recommendations. As a First Sergeant, you should expect a reduction in rank every time, and have the reduced rank in your pocket. If the Soldier is reduced "effective immediately," change the rank before the Soldier leaves the office.

UCMJ should be a swift process, do not take your time with this. Discipline in the military is critical to maintain good order and conduct. If the Soldier is a good Soldier that simply made a mistake then they will understand what you have to do. When considering recommendation for punishment take in account the Soldiers career and propensity for disciplinary issues.

Leadership Theories

Every leader has their own leadership style. In order to improve, we identify our own strengths and weaknesses and make changes that will have a positive impact on our Soldiers and mission accomplishment. I will discuss some theories in leadership that, when compared to others, might help you identify and improve your leadership style. There are many leadership theories; here I will discuss some of the major categories one might fall under.

Trait Theory

Trait theory assumes that people inherit certain qualities and traits that make them better suited for leadership. Trait theories often identify particular personality or behavioral characteristics shared by leaders. If particular traits are key features of leadership, then how do we explain people who possess those qualities but are not leaders? This question is one of the difficulties in using trait theories to explain leadership.

Contingency Theory

Contingency theories of leadership focus on particular variables related to the environment that might determine which particular style of leadership is best suited for the situation. According to this theory, no leadership style is best in all situations. Success depends upon a number of variables, including the leadership style, qualities of the followers and aspects of the situation.

Situational Theory

Much like Contingency theories, Situational theories propose that leaders choose the best course of action based upon situational variables. Different styles of leadership may be more appropriate for certain types of decision-making.

Behavioral Theory

Unlike the Trait theory, Behavioral theories of leadership are based upon the belief that great leaders are made, not born. Rooted in behaviorism, this leadership theory focuses on the actions of leaders, not on mental qualities or internal states. According to this theory, people can *learn* to become leaders through teaching and observation.

Participative Theory

Participative leadership theories suggest that the ideal leadership style is one that takes the input of others into account. These leaders encourage participation and contributions from group members and help group members feel more relevant and committed to the decision-making process. In participative theories, however, the leader retains the right to allow the input of others.

Management Theory

Management theories, also known as transactional theories, focus on the role of supervision, organization and group performance. These theories base leadership on a system of rewards and punishments. Managerial theories are often used in business; when employees are successful, they are rewarded; when they fail, they are reprimanded or punished. This mimics the foundation of leadership in the military.

Relationship Theory

Relationship theories, also known as transformational theories, focus upon the connections formed between leaders and followers. Transformational leaders motivate and inspire people by helping group members see the importance and higher good of the task. These leaders are focused on the performance of group members, but also want each person to fulfill his or her potential. Leaders with this style often have high ethical and moral standards.

In summary, no leader will fall into any single category. The leader that is adaptable and can learn from their mistakes go on to be successful. Use these theories to understand your subordinates, and again, do not be so quick to judge a subordinate's decision-making process.

Safety Brief

You and your Commander are responsible for the safety of your Soldiers. Every Friday one of you will give the safety briefing. Just because you do it every week, DO NOT minimize the importance of it.

If you drink "don't drive" / if you drive "don't drink"

Forty percent of all vehicle related fatalities involve alcohol. This is a huge problem in the military, do whatever you have to in order to get your Soldiers to call for a ride. It may save their life or career if they are lucky.

POV safety, wear seatbelts, don't speed, and don't drive sleepy

The other sixty percent of POV fatalities are caused by carelessness and irrational behavior. Keep them alert / keep them alive.

Let me bail you out before you go to jail

I tell my Soldiers this every Friday, once they are in jail, have a positive UA or have an alcohol related incident, it's too late and my hands are tied. Refer to the zero tolerance list, which means there are no exceptions even for the Soldier of the Year. Encourage your Soldiers to come forward with their problems so they can get help.

Don't do drugs / Stay away from spice and bath salt

This stuff will kill them. It is a growing trend because for some reason Soldiers think that some homemade off the shelf drugs are undetectable. This may have been true at first but the labs have modified their system to detect it.

Keep the barracks clean / CDR can initiate H&W at any time

Personally go through the barracks during payday activities, it is a great tool for keeping the barracks clean. SQD Leaders and PSGs should be checking barracks often anyway.

Avoid domestic violence / walk away

If your Soldier gets physical at all, even to defend themselves, it is too late. They need to get away from the situation and call their supervisor immediately.

Suicide is a selfish act, look for indicators in others

This is a very serious issue; jokes about suicide should not be tolerated! Learn who your high risk Soldiers are and try to mitigate any situation that might result in harm to them or others.

Safe Sex

Single Soldiers need to be aware that there are sexually transmitted diseases out there that will kill you. AIDS, for example, can take up to five years to completely destroy your immune system and in some cases leave you to die a slow horrible death.

Motorcycle Safety / wear proper gear and stay alert

Even if you do not own a motorcycle, you should understand the danger your Soldiers face. Enforce local and state law and encourage safe driving.

Swimming / need lifeguard on duty / avoid unauthorized areas

Mostly in summer, months Soldiers should be reminded the dangers of drinking and swimming. In addition, if there is a fatality resulting from violations in safety guidelines their family may not receive the life insurance benefit.

Weapon Safety / keep guns in arms room / and be safe hunting

Most military installations do not allow concealed weapons to be carried. Stress maturity and precaution when handling weapons systems. Most states require you to be 21 in order to purchase firearms.

Keep up the good work – stay motivated

I like to close out my safety briefs on a positive note. Through positive reinforcement, Soldiers are more likely to take initiative in the absence of orders.

Sexual Assault Prevention and Response Program

Policy, DoD Guidance, Regulations, and Memorandums

The Sexual Assault Prevention and Response Program reinforces the Army's commitment to eliminate incidents of sexual assault through a comprehensive policy that centers on awareness and prevention, training and education, victim advocacy, response, reporting, and accountability. Army policy promotes sensitive care and confidential reporting for victims of sexual assault and accountability for those who commit these crimes.

The goals of the Sexual Assault Prevention and Response Program are:

- Create a climate that minimizes sexual assault incidents, which affect Army personnel, Army civilians, and family members, and, if an incident should occur, ensure that victims and subjects are treated according to Army policy.

- Create a climate that encourages victims to report incidents of sexual assault without fear.

- Establish sexual assault prevention training and awareness programs to educate Soldiers.

- Ensure sensitive and comprehensive treatment to restore victims' health and well-being.

- Ensure leaders understand their roles and responsibilities regarding response to sexual assault victims, thoroughly investigate allegations of sexual assault, and take appropriate administrative and disciplinary action.

Reporting options: Restricted / Unrestricted Reporting

Sexual Assault is the most under reported crime in our society and in the military. While the Department of Defense prefers complete reporting of sexual assaults to activate both victims' services and law enforcement actions, it recognizes that some victims desire only medical and support services and no command or law enforcement involvement. The Department believes its first priority is for victims to be protected, treated with dignity and respect, and to receive the medical treatment, care and counseling that they deserve. Under DoD's Confidentiality Policy, sexual assault victims are offered two reporting options-Restricted reporting and Unrestricted reporting.

Understanding DoD's Confidentiality Policy

DoD's Confidentiality policy permits victims of sexual assault to report the crime to specified individuals who can then ensure the victim receives medical care, treatment and counseling without notifying command or law enforcement officials. Covered individuals include the Sexual Assault Response Coordinator (SARC); Victim Advocates (VA); healthcare providers; and chaplains. For purposes of public safety and command responsibility, the SARC will notify the installation commander that an assault has occurred and provide details that will not identify the victim. (See Directive-Type Memorandum, Confidentiality Policy for Victims of Sexual Assault (JTF-SAPR-009), for complete details).

This policy provides victims some personal space and time, and increased control over the release and management of their personal information. This hopefully empowers them to seek relevant information and support to make more informed decisions about participating in the criminal investigation. Jurisdictions with similar policies have found that confidentiality actually leads to increased reporting rates. Even if the victim chooses not to pursue an official investigation, this additional reporting avenue gives commanders a clearer picture of the sexual violence within their command, and enhances a commander's ability to provide an environment that is safe and contributes to the well-being and mission-readiness of all of its members.

Restricted Reporting

This option is recommended for victims of sexual assault who wish to confidentially disclose the crime to specifically identified individuals and receive medical treatment and counseling without triggering the official investigative process. Service members who are sexually assaulted and desire restricted reporting under this policy must report the assault to a Sexual Assault Response Coordinator (SARC), Victim Advocate (VA), or a healthcare provider.

As provided for above, victims may also discuss the assault with a chaplain. Discussing the assault with a chaplain is not a restricted report under this policy; it is a communication that may be protected under the Military Rules of Evidence

(MRE) or applicable statues and regulations. The restricted reporting process does not affect any privilege recognized under the MRE. This policy on restricted reporting is in addition to the current protections afforded by privileged communications with a chaplain, and does not alter or affect those protections.

Healthcare providers will initiate the appropriate care and treatment, and report the sexual assault to the SARC in lieu of reporting the assault to law enforcement or the command. Upon notification of a reported sexual assault, the SARC will immediately assign a VA to the victim. The assigned VA will provide accurate information on the process of restricted vice unrestricted reporting.

At the victim's discretion/request, an appropriately trained healthcare provider shall conduct a sexual assault forensic examination (SAFE), which may include the collection of evidence. In the absence of a DoD provider, the service member will be referred to an appropriate civilian facility for the SAFE.

Who may make a Restricted Report

Restricted reporting is available at this time to military personnel of the Armed Forces and Military Dependents 18 years of age and older who are eligible for treatment in the military healthcare system, who were victims of sexual assault perpetrated by someone other than a spouse or intimate partner. Military personnel include members on active duty and members of the Reserve component (Reserve and National Guard). NG and Reserve Component members will be eligible to receive limited SAPR support services from a SARC and a SAPR VA and are eligible to file a Restricted or Unrestricted Report if they are reporting a sexual assault that occurred prior to, or while not performing active service or inactive training. SAPR Services are those that are provided by a SARC or SAPR VA.

Whether they file a Restricted or Unrestricted Report, members of the Reserve Components shall have access to medical treatment and counseling for injuries and illness incurred from a sexual assault inflicted upon a Service member when performing active duty service and during inactive duty training. Medical entitlements remain dependent on a Line of Duty determination as to whether or not the sexual assault incident occurred in an active duty or inactive duty training status. However, regardless of their duty status at the time that the sexual assault incident occurred, or at the time that they are seeking SAPR services, Reserve Component members can elect either the Restricted or Unrestricted Reporting option and have access to the SAPR services of a SARC and a SAPR VA.

At this time, Retired members of any component are not eligible for a restricted report and Department of Defense civilian employees are not eligible.

Restricted Reporting example

- Service Member Smith arrives at the base medical emergency room and reports she has been sexually assaulted. Healthcare providers immediately notify the SARC and begin any appropriate emergency medical treatment.

- The SARC assigns a VA to assist Service Member Smith. The VA meets Service Member Smith at the hospital and explains the Unrestricted/Restricted Reporting options and the processes associated with each, to include applicable pros/cons.

- Service Member Smith elects the Restricted Reporting option.

- Service Member Smith is asked if she would like a forensic examination, and she agrees.

- The VA advises the Healthcare Provider that Service Member Smith has elected the Restricted Reporting option and would like a SAFE.

- Forensic evidence of the assault is collected and preserved in a non-personally identifying manner.

- The Healthcare Provider determines and schedules follow-up medical treatment as appropriate.

- The VA advises the SARC that Service Member Smith has elected the Restricted Reporting option.

- Within 24 hours of Service Member Smith's restricted report, the SARC will inform the Installation Commander that an assault has occurred, and provide the Commander with non-identifying personal information/details related to the sexual assault allegation. This information includes rank; gender; age; race; service; date; time and/or location. Information is disclosed in a manner that preserves the victim's anonymity. Careful consideration of which details to include is of particular significance at installations or other locations where there are a limited number of minority females or female officers assigned.

- The Installation Commander may notify the Criminal Investigators. However, no criminal investigation will be initiated unless originated from another source or the victim elects to come forward via unrestricted reporting. The Installation Commander identifies trends and responds appropriately (i.e. increased security patrols, enhanced education and training, enhanced environmental and safety measures) to prevent further sexual assaults.

- The SARC maintains information regarding the number of sexual assaults for both unrestricted and restricted reports. Restricted report numbers will be included in the annual report. The SARC will also capture trends and perform trend analysis. SARC awareness of trends will be a first line of defense against a potential serial assailant. The SARC can at any time return to Service Member Smith to ask if she is willing to reconsider her restricted reporting decision given the potential of a serial offender.

- The VA maintains communication and contact with the victim as needed for continued victim support.

Considerations when electing a Restricted Reporting decision

Benefits

- You receive appropriate medical treatment, advocacy, and counseling.

- Provides some personal space and time to consider your options and to begin the healing process.

- Empowers you to seek relevant information and support to make more informed decisions about participating in the criminal investigation.

- You control the release and management of your personal information.

- You decide whether and when to move forward with initiating an investigation.

Limitations

- Your assailant remains unpunished and capable of assaulting other victims.

- You cannot receive a military protective order.

- You will continue to have contact with your assailant, if he/she is in your organization or billeted with you.

- Evidence from the crime scene where the assault occurred will be lost, and the official investigation, should you switch to an unrestricted report, will likely encounter significant obstacles.

- You will not be able to discuss the assault with anyone, to include your friends, without imposing an obligation on them to report the crime. The only exceptions would be chaplains, designated healthcare providers, your assigned victim advocate, and the sexual assault response coordinator.

- You will be ineligible to invoke the collateral misconduct provision of the Department's sexual assault policy in the event that your command learns that you had been engaged in some form of misconduct at the time you were assaulted.

Unrestricted Reporting

This option is recommended for victims of sexual assault who desire medical treatment, counseling and an official investigation of the crime. When selecting unrestricted reporting, you should use current reporting channels, e.g. chain of command, law enforcement or report the incident to the Sexual Assault Response Coordinator (SARC), or request healthcare providers to notify law enforcement. Upon notification of a reported sexual assault, the SARC will immediately assign a Victim Advocate (VA). At the victim's discretion/request, the healthcare provider shall conduct a sexual assault forensic examination (SAFE), which may include the collection of evidence. Details regarding the incident will be limited to only those personnel who have a legitimate need to know.

Unrestricted Reporting example

- Service Member Smith arrives at the base medical emergency room and reports she has been sexually assaulted. Healthcare providers immediately notify the Sexual Assault Response Coordinator (SARC) and begin administration of any emergency medical treatment as appropriate.

- The SARC assigns a Victim Advocate (VA) to assist Service Member Smith. The VA meets Service Member Smith at the hospital, explains the Unrestricted/Restricted Reporting options and processes associated with each to include applicable pros/cons.

- Service Member Smith elects the Unrestricted Reporting option.

- The VA immediately notifies the appropriate Criminal Investigative Service and the victim's unit commander.

- Criminal Investigators arrive and begin the investigation.

- Service Member Smith is asked if she would like a SAFE, and she agrees.

- The VA advises the Healthcare Provider that Service Member Smith has elected the Unrestricted Reporting option and would like a SAFE.

- Forensic evidence of the assault is collected by healthcare providers, and at its conclusion, criminal investigators take chain of custody.

- The Healthcare Provider determines and schedules follow-up medical treatment as appropriate.

- The VA advises the SARC that Service Member Smith has elected the Unrestricted Reporting option.

- In addition to any current existing channels of notification, within 24 hours of Service Member Smith's Unrestricted report, the SARC will inform the Installation Commander that an assault has occurred, and provide the Commander with the details of the assault.

- The SARC maintains information regarding the number of sexual assaults for both unrestricted and restricted reports. Restricted report numbers will be included in the annual report. The SARC will also capture trends and perform trend analysis.

- The VA maintains communications and contact with victim as needed for continued victim support.

SHARP Conclusion

Having dealt with this topic on a very personal matter I can tell you that in any instance it is NOT to be minimized. The threats are very real and have lifelong consequences. You as a leader have a responsibility to know policy and procedure and be able to effectively implement measures that prevent this type of behavior. On the same note, do not jump to conclusion when receiving reports. Take immediate action then gather all information before persecuting someone. This is a very sensitive topic in today's military with high visibility throughout the government. With this type of scrutiny commanders do not want to give the impression, they are siding with the accused. It is your duty to set your emotions aside and provide a clear train of thought for your commander to fall back on.

Link to SHARP Company Commanders Guidebook (September 2013)

https://www.us.army.mil/suite/kc/41160047

Training

Introduction

I cannot begin to stress the importance of a well-trained unit. This is a First Sergeants priority when charged with unit readiness. I could probably write an entire book on training but just like every other chapter in this book; I will give you the essential basics. Training guidance changes often, therefore you as a leader should always make sure you have the most up to date and accurate information when validating your junior NCOs training plans. There are several factors to take into consideration when preparing for realistic, challenging, and required training. The latest Army reference for training is *ADRP 7-0 (23 AUG 2012)*, if you have not completely wrapped your head around this doctrine you need to get a copy and read it! At some point in your career you will hear the term "engaged leader", this manual not only covers training but developing leaders.

USAREC Reg 350-1, 2-10. First sergeants
First sergeants are the companies training expert. First sergeants:
a. Advise the commander on training priorities, assist in the identification of training needs, and direct and monitor the delivery of all training.
b. Monitor the company's self-development and physical fitness training.
c. Monitor the RDP and ATP and evaluate recruiters' progress throughout the entire program (see app E).
d. Manage the company's NCOPD.
e. Ensure Soldiers are mentally and physically prepared for professional development courses.

Mandatory Training in Units

Ref. (AR350-1 04 August 2012)

a. Because of their importance to overall force readiness, training on certain subject matter is required as mandatory training and will be recorded at part of the ITR.

b. Proficiency in mandatory training subject matter is required for all members of units, regardless of branch/career field or rank/grade. Mandatory training requirements are limited to those subject areas directed by law and HQDA. The HQDA, DCS, G–3/5/7 maintains centralized control over mandatory directed training requirements and reviews them semiannually. Appendix G and table G–1 summarize mandatory training requirements for units. This training will be documented in DTMS and the ITR.

Figure 11 [AR 350-1 Table G-1 Mandatory Training Requirements in Units]

Table G–1
Mandatory training requirements in units

Subject	Reference	Proponent	Frequency
Antiterrorism training	AR 525–13	PMG	A
Army physical fitness training	AR 350–1	HQDA, DCS, G–3/5/7	O
Army Substance Abuse Program	AR 600–85	HQDA, DCS, G–1	I/A/R
Army Suicide Prevention Program	AR 600–63	HQDA, DCS, G–1	A/P/R
Army Traffic Safety Training Program	AR 385–10	HQDA, ACSIM	I
Army Warrior Training	https://atiam.train.army.mil/soldierPortal/	HQDA, DCS, G–3/5/7	A
CBRN Defense training	AR 350–1	TRADOC	A
Combating Trafficking in Persons (CTIP) Program	http://www.combat-trafficking.army.mil/	ASA(M&RA)	A/P
Composite Risk Management	AR 385–10	TRADOC	O
Cultural awareness training	AR 350–1 Chapter 8	TRADOC	P
Employment and reemployment rights (RC only)	DODI 1205.12	HQDA, DCS, G–1	A/P/R
Equal Opportunity Program	AR 600–20	HQDA, DCS, G–1	S
Ethics (see details below)	DOD 5500.7–R	TJAG	Initial entry
Fraternization	AR 600–20	HQDA, DCS, G–1	A
Law of War / Detainee Ops	DODD 2311.01E	TJAG	A/P
Modern Army Combatives Program	AR 350–1	TRADOC (USACS)	O
Operational security (OPSEC)	AR 530–1	HQDA, DCS, G–3/5/7	I/A/R
Personnel Recovery	AR 350–1	HQDA, DCS, G–3/5/7	A
Prevention of Sexual Harassment	AR 600–20	HQDA, DCS, G–1	S
Preventive measures against disease and injury	AR 40–5	TSG	P
Resilience training	www.battlemind.army.mil	MEDCOM	P/R
SAEDA	AR 381–12	HQDA, DCS, G–2	A
Sexual Assault Prevention and Response Program	AR 600–20	HQDA, DCS, G–1	A/P/R
Weapons qualification	DA Pam 350–38	HQDA, DCS, G–3/5/7	S (AA) A (RC)

Legend for Table G-1:
The following codes establish the frequency at which training is to be conducted:
A: Annual. Trained annually.
I: Inprocessing. Required whenever an individual is assigned to a new unit.
O: Ongoing. Continuous training, not a single event.
P: Pre-Deployment. Addressed before unit is deployed on an operational mission.
R: Redeployment. Addressed upon redeployment from an operational mission.
S: Semiannual. Trained twice per year.
Notes:
[1] *Published pre-deployment training guidance supersedes training requirement frequency contained herein.

Preparation for Training

Before I begin ANY training from running a weapons qualification range to a simple slide presentation on leadership development. There is one thing I always take into consideration first, and that is safety. A few documents that I recommend be on site during training are the, *Composite Risk Management Worksheet CDTCMD Form 385-1-R-E, Your Task, Conditions, and Standards* (preferably on display) and the reference for the training being given.

Figure 12 [CDTCMD Form 385-1-R-E. (REV JULY 07) Composite Risk Management Worksheet]

COMPOSITE RISK MANAGEMENT WORKSHEET
(CDTCMD Reg 385-10; proponent agency is Cadet Command Safety)

1. Organization and Unit Location:				2. Page ___ of ___	
3. Mission/Task:			4. Begin Date:	5. End Date:	6. Date Prepared:

7. Operational Phase in which the Mission/Task will be conducted:

8. Tasks	9. Identify Hazards	10. Initial Risk Level	11. Develop Controls	12. Residual Risk Level	13. Implement Controls ("How To")	14. Who/How Supervised	15. Was Control Effective?

LOW (L)   MODERATE (M)   HIGH (H)   EXTREMELY HIGH (E)

16. Determine Overall Mission/Task Risk Level After Countermeasures Are Implemented: (Circle Highest Remaining Risk Level)

17. Medical Support: Advanced Trauma Life Support (ATLS) is required within 1 hour. On-site Medical Support provided (Circle one): Doctor/Nurse   Combat Lifesaver   None   Medic

18. Prepared by (Rank, Last Name, Duty Position)

19. Reviewed by Action Officer/Commander: (Rank, Last Name, Duty Position and Signature):

20. Risk Decision Authority (Signature Block and Signature):

Extremely High Risk: Not Applicable for Cadet Command
High Risk: CG or DCG
Moderate Risk: Brigade Cdr (0-6). At LDAC, LTC/ JCLC – Region Cdr or CofS
Low Risk: Battalion Cdr. At LDAC, LTC/ Commandant– Committee Chief or Regimental Cdr/TAC Officer

CDTCMD Form 385-1-R-E, (REV JULY 07)   Risk Assessment and Risk Management Countermeasure Worksheets in CC Reg 145-3 are OBSOLETE

Training Models

ADRP 7-0, 3-59. *Training models can provide a framework for planning and managing training events. Training models, such as the eight-step training model, are only guides and not lock-step processes. They can be useful, but they are, effectively, just modifications of either the MDMP or TLP.*

The Eight-Step Training Model

It is a simple, progressive checklist approach to plan, prepare, execute, and assess training. The model helps commanders organize and record planning progression. This kind of detail ensures proper preparation for training and maximizes the efficient and effective use of time and resources. Note: DTMS will be used by commanders to plan, track, and review training events.

1. *Plan the Training*

2. *Train and Certify Leaders*

3. *Select the Training Site*

4. *Issue a Complete Order for Training*

5. *Rehearse*

6. *Execute*

7. *After-Action Review (AAR)*

8. *Retrain*

Step 1: Plan the training. During this step, leaders assess the unit's performance to evaluate the training level and shortfalls; develop specific, obtainable training objectives; allocate time for the specified training; create scenarios and instructions to support the training objectives; identify required resources, including training sites and trainers; use composite risk management (CRM); and develop training support plans, thereby establishing the groundwork for high- quality training.

Step 2: Train and certify leaders. The "train-the-trainer" concept ensures those responsible for training, whether they are civilians or Soldiers, are qualified, knowledgeable of the subject matter, and able to provide proper instruction. This step ensures leaders understand and conduct training according to established doctrine and best business practices. Experienced and successful recruiters and leaders are a valuable training resource whose experiences can contribute to best train the recruiting force.

Step 3: Select the training site. Leaders should ensure selected sites can adequately support the proposed training and desired training objectives. During this step, leaders at all levels should check to ensure all resources, training aids, and training support plans are properly coordinated and prepared for execution. Modifications to the plan may occur during this step to maximize training effectiveness. Training that is not properly planned, coordinated, and supported with adequate resources wastes valuable training time and resources and should not be performed.

Step 4: Issue a complete order for training. Vital to this step is a clear understanding by all of exactly what the training will accomplish, how the unit will accomplish it, what resources will be needed, and who is responsible. Leaders should ensure subordinates have all available information to adequately perform the training mission.

Step 5: Rehearse. Rehearsals are critical to the execution of any plan. All those involved in the training event should conduct a rehearsal to ensure synchronization and preparation of the plan. Leaders should supervise rehearsals to ensure those responsible for the training are prepared to conduct efficient, organized, and effective needs-based training.

Step 6: Execute. Commanders should ensure training occurs on schedule. This helps commanders minimize training distracters and allows them to assess the training level.

Step 7: AAR. After training is completed, commanders should review the training objectives; assess the training level in respect to the objectives; and obtain lessons learned, to improve training and unit tactics, techniques, and procedures (TTP). Commanders should record lessons learned for future training use and inclusion in the unit's standing operating procedure (SOP). Commanders must continuously assess unit performance during actual operations to identify recruiting performance shortfalls. Shortfalls attributed to a Soldier's lack of skill or knowledge must be addressed through needs-based training.

Step 8: Retrain. This step is often neglected because of limited time or resources or other pressing tasks. This step, however, is usually the most critical. Training instills competency and confidence in Soldiers, units, and leaders; and enables the unit to complete its mission. Commanders should honestly assess their units and ensure they train and retrain until the standard is met. Clear objectives, effective training, and continuous assessment are the keys to success.

Example Training Story Board

A training storyboard like the example in *Figure 13* is a great way to sum up a training event. It gives an overview of the training area and validation criteria.

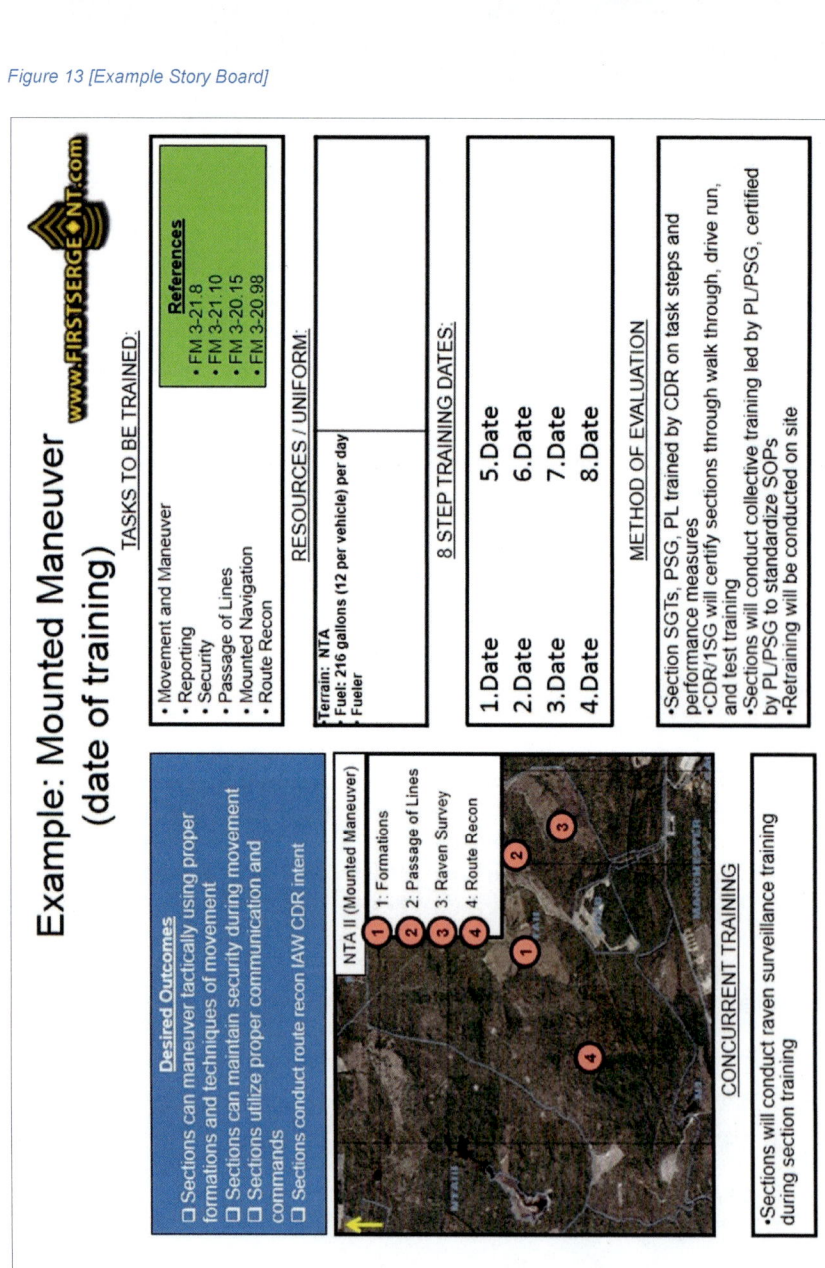

Figure 13 [Example Story Board]

Example: Mounted Maneuver (date of training)

TASKS TO BE TRAINED:
- Movement and Maneuver
- Reporting
- Security
- Passage of Lines
- Mounted Navigation
- Route Recon

References
- FM 3-21.8
- FM 3-21.10
- FM 3-20.15
- FM 3-20.98

RESOURCES / UNIFORM:
Terrain: NTA
Fuel: 216 gallons (12 per vehicle) per day
Fueler

8 STEP TRAINING DATES:
1. Date
2. Date
3. Date
4. Date
5. Date
6. Date
7. Date
8. Date

METHOD OF EVALUATION
- Section SGTs, PSG, PL trained by CDR on task steps and performance measures
- CDR/1SG will certify sections through walk through, drive run, and test training
- Sections will conduct collective training led by PL/PSG, certified by PL/PSG to standardize SOPs
- Retraining will be conducted on site

Desired Outcomes
☐ Sections can maneuver tactically using proper formations and techniques of movement
☐ Sections can maintain security during movement
☐ Sections utilize proper communication and commands
☐ Sections conduct route recon IAW CDR intent

NTA II (Mounted Maneuver)
1: Formations
2: Passage of Lines
3: Raven Survey
4: Route Recon

CONCURRENT TRAINING
- Sections will conduct raven surveillance training during section training

www.FIRSTSERGE★NT.com

42

Responsibilities

Overview

Purpose

To identify and define the priorities and standards expected by the unit 1SG.

Scope

This section provides a general outline as far as expectations and conduct of the senior Non-Commissioned Officers in your unit.

General

You and the Commander make up the command team and your success as a unit depends on your ability to lead and work together. Let the Commander command the unit and issue intent and guidance, but it is you whom she/he depend on most to ensure that it runs based on those instructions. You, along with the NCOs, are directly responsible for the daily operation of the unit. You will be directly responsible for everything the company does or fails to do.

Teamwork

You and your Commander depend heavily upon one another as you build, re-fit, re-train, and re-focus the unit. As you learn how your company runs and operates, keep your Commander informed on all facets of its leaders and its Soldiers. You must place aside your differences, if you happen to have any, IOT execute what is expected of the command team. You are responsible for the daily operations, however, your Commander is responsible for the company's mission, and therefore no decision that directly affects the mission should be made without their input. This includes labor issues, equipment allocations, priorities of work, and Soldier absence. You two make up the command team and together you will lead your Soldiers to war if the need arises.

Commander's Intent

Never leave their office confused. If you do not understand or are unsure about their guidance, ask them. You must be on the same sheet of music 100% of the time, as I said before One Voice. This does not exclude you from voicing your opinions. You can disagree, but it should always occur behind closed doors. Respect is more than just "Yes, sir!" If their intent is ever unclear, make it known so they can ensure their concepts are properly communicated. You should defend and support them (unless evidence proves otherwise). Nothing can destroy your command climate faster than a lack of mutual support. No one is to come between you, and once the final order is given, unless illegal, immoral or unethical, it will be executed.

Conditions set by the 1SG

Competence

- You must be tactically and technically proficient both in garrison and field activities in order to provide guidance to the unit on all skills applicable to your mission. You must be an expert in your trade. These skill sets are what you must draw upon when providing the CDR guidance on meeting the unit's mission.
- As the senior NCO, you must remain proficient in your assigned duty MOS as well as those other MOSs assigned to your unit.
- Competence stands for the desire to seek continued improvement. Once the bar is set and surpassed, raise it higher.
- All tasks must be accomplished 100%. If you fail to complete your mission, it means you may produce failure in the units you support or protect. If failure appears to be eminent, notify your Commander ASAP so you can adjust your plans.

Physical Fitness & Military Bearing

- The 1SG sets the standards for the Soldiers to follow. You will maintain a 270 APFT average (or higher) and will train the unit to do the same. You must always be out front setting the example and giving 110%!
- You are the owner of the physical fitness program. In an Army at war, fitness is more than push-ups, sit-ups and the 2-mile run. Good PT

programs include ruck-marches, combatives, obstacle courses— they are battle focused! Think out of the box, but maintain standards. My only real guidance with the PT program is that it is executed at the lowest level possible to afford your junior leaders opportunities to plan and excel...outside of that, it is your plan. Soldiers that do not conduct P.T. in the morning should make every effort to be present during remedial P.T. hours.

- Appearance and Bearing should never be lacking. AR 670-1 must be adhered to and enforced. Always maintain a sharp military appearance and make every attempt to exceed the standard.
- Respect seniors and subordinates alike. Avoid using "They said" or the "the Boss said". Talking down on others only fosters contempt within the ranks and breeds problems. Never complain or criticize other officers or NCOs in front of your Soldiers. Gossiping by the senior leadership will destroy your command like a rotting cancer.
- Your Soldiers should maintain basic customs and courtesies at all times. Soldiers should stand at attention or parade rest when being addressed by a superior. Leaders should call the room to attention or "at ease" when the 1SG or Commander are entering the room to begin a meeting. Soldiers should call the company to attention or "at ease" when the 1SG or Commander arrive or depart for the day. These basic standards of customs and courtesies are marks of a unit's discipline and should be adhered to.
- PT Failures and Weight control. If your Soldiers cannot maintain their weight within allowable standards or cannot pass the Army Physical Fitness Test, they must be enrolled in a remedial PT program.

Leading

- Lead by example and always do the right thing. You will be under observation at all times. You cannot expect Soldiers to follow or enforce the standards, unless you exemplify them.
- Your actions set the tone for the unit both on and off duty. You may drink, but do not abuse alcohol. Drinking and driving is a zero tolerance item. Maintain your finances. If you drive a motorcycle, operate it within established laws.
- Be honest in word and deed. Have integrity and be a professional.
- Soldiers must be encouraged to use the NCO support channel appropriately. Be an approachable person but do not allow Soldiers to see you without going through their chain of command.
- Soldiers come first, but not at the cost of teaching, them what right looks like. You are there to ensure the unit prepares for and executes its

wartime mission and that the sons and daughters of this nation return home safe.
- Keep your Soldiers informed. Ensure the current training schedules and the company quarterly training calendars are posted on the company and section boards.

Training

- Get involved in the training of all your Soldiers. Ensure all training and tasks are conducted in the Task, Conditions, and Standards format. All lesson plans and actions should be doctrinally correct, easily referenced, and rehearsed prior to execution. This includes PT, SGT's Time Training, Marksmanship Training, Airborne Operations, or any other Individual Training. Training is not read from a book. Training is taught in the classroom and executed at field sites and in the motor pool. Your focus should always be on your real-world mission.
- You must constantly focus on the development of your subordinates. You should delegate and provide guidance, then supervise and inspect. You may have to accept less than perfect products at times in the interest of training subordinates. Train, AAR / counsel, and retrain your subordinates.
- Implement an NCOPD program that builds upon itself. Ensure the NCO leaders understand the importance of complete, concise counseling, NCOER's, awards, punishment, college advantages, the AAR process, Lessons Learned, etc. You should host at least one NCOPD per month.
- Do not accept dental appointments, legal appointments, or other personal appointments as valid reasons for missing key training. Never make your Soldiers execute a task in combat for the first time.
- Be present at and inspect training; positively and proactively assessing, analyzing, and AAR as appropriate. Do not allow yourself to be consumed by the "Paper War" and fail to be at training.
- Realistic, tough, and demanding training develops confidence; it is the best-proven way to prepare your Soldiers.

Responsibility & Accountability

- All personnel should be accounted for 100% of the time. This includes PT, schools, details, training etc. Expect an honest day's work from all of your Soldiers and leaders. When Soldiers are not at the right place, at the right time, in the right uniform, you should expect written counseling / documentation to cover that incident - retraining is not only acceptable it is expected.

- The AAA-162 is your business. Learn the process and cover every Soldier with your Commander.
- Ensure all leaders and members of the company are maintaining their equipment appropriately. Equipment inadequacies should never prevent you from executing your mission. All Soldiers should utilize proper PMCS by the book and learn how to safely utilize their equipment.
- All equipment should be accounted for in garrison and field environments. The primary hand receipt holders in accordance with the command supply program should account for all property.
- Visit the Arms Room weekly. The standards are no dust, no rust or carbon and a light coat of oil on all weapons. Your Soldiers will rely on these weapons in war; maintain them as if they were your last defense.

Administration

- UCMJ / Admin separations – advise, recommend, initiate, and ensure all information is present to make fair decisions, protect Soldier's rights, and supervise any "corrective" training imposed. Leaders make administrative recommendations and Commanders make administrative decisions.
- Ensure your Soldier's files are straight. Personnel data sheets updated, high dollar item sheets updated, counseling completed at least monthly, all pay issues are squared away, PCS awards are submitted three months prior to PCS and NCOERs are done at least 35 days prior to PCS. Ensure your counseling packets are uniform and complete. Ensure your promotion packets clearly outline the capabilities of your future leaders.
- Ensure the Family Care Plans and SRP packets are up-to-date.
- Ensure the company Dental stats (Class I, II, III, IV) and MEDPROS status is monitored for 100% accuracy. These are clear indicators of your unit's readiness and require weekly review.
- Ensure the following monthly reports are completed on time and to standard: AAA-162, UCFR, C10, C01, Barracks roster, NCOER rating scheme, and unit MOSI (manning report).
- Monitor the UCFR and LESs monthly to ensure there are no issues that may affect your Soldiers or their loved ones. Ensure your Soldiers are receiving the pay and allowances they are authorized.
- Ensure your company alert roster is updated at least once a month, or more if necessary.
- A solid sponsorship program for incoming Soldiers is critical to their integration into the unit. Ensure your policies are briefed and understood by the company and by the incoming Soldiers.

Discipline

Train discipline and enforce discipline every day in every task. Discipline must be your Hallmark, a part of your normal daily business. Disciplined Soldiers and leaders do their duties promptly and effectively in response to orders, or even in the absence of orders. Soldiers and leaders with self-discipline do what they need to do regardless of supervision, stress, exhaustion, or other conditions. You set the example and tone for discipline in your unit. Areas that provide immediate discipline indicators are:
- Military Courtesy and Bearing
- Uniformity: enforce standards, know AR 670-1, 672-5-1, FM 22-5
- Attention to Detail Items: Accountability, Details, Rosters, Schedules, Information/Policy Boards etc.

Display a positive mental attitude. Love Soldiering, always mentor and retrain. Be proactive and make things happen, it is contagious. Remember, false motivation is better than no motivation at all...
Your time should not be consumed with tasks that would be transparent in a disciplined unit.

Indicators of Poor Leadership

- Lack of discipline, military appearance and bearing
- Failure to complete a mission, especially when you have the ability to accomplish it.
- Failure to report when the mission is not going to be met.
- Piss poor, unplanned, un-resourced training that wastes Soldier's time, i.e. throwing an NCO in front of formation to lead PT without notice.
- Failing to disseminate information; training schedules, PT plan, etc.
- Lack of accountability and stewardship for Army property.
- Junior leaders making decisions that goes against known intent and guidance from senior leaders because of laziness or lack of motivation. The "I know what he said, but we can do it tomorrow" attitude.
- Leaders knowing what is wrong and not fixing it.
- Senior leaders having to make on-the-spot corrections that a junior leader should have corrected.
- Whining and excuses—from leaders. Whining is a lack of professionalism.
- Lack of organization in work areas. Messy work areas are clear indicators of a lack of discipline and a lack in efficiency. Work areas and offices must be professionally maintained at all times.
- Leadership Not Following Up or Checking progress.

- Lack of safety and failure to use prescribed personal protective equipment (PPE).

Indicators of Outstanding Leadership

- Disciplined, motivated, and hardworking Soldiers giving 110%, earning their paycheck, and making a difference
- "Catching" leaders doing the right thing and training Soldiers beyond established standard, not just when they are expecting it
- Maintaining good property accountability through effective use of hand receipts and shortage annexes
- Maintaining a physical fitness program that is innovative and focuses on long term improvement
- Planned, resourced, and challenging GO-TO-WAR training!
- Maintaining a sense of humor
- Acknowledging that mistakes happen, accept them and drive on
- Soldiers and Leaders making on-the-spot corrections
- Serving with professionals you can count on—all the time

Zero Tolerance Items

- SEXUAL HARASSMENT
- FRATERNIZATION
- EQUAL OPPORTUNITY
- DRUGS
- DRUNK DRIVING
- INTEGRITY VIOLATION

100% Your Responsibility

- Individual Training and Schools
- Unit Manning
- Counseling and Promotions
- NCOPD
- Physical Training
- Individual Equipment Management
- Soldiers Living Areas
- Tasking Management
- Weapons Assignments and Qualification
- Standards!

Counseling Formats

Lower enlisted initial

Possible Key Points for Discussion:

Attitude

Be positive and have fun. Do not get into the bad habit of complaining all the time, particularly in front of the people who work for you. Instead, try to fix the problem you are complaining about. If it is worth complaining about, it is worth doing something about.

AWOL Prevention

Soldiers go AWOL for numerous reasons. Often it is because the Soldier faces an urgent situation and a perception that the leadership will be unresponsive. It is the responsibility of leaders to take positive action to resolve Soldier's problems and to maintain a climate that makes it easier for a Soldier to turn to his leadership for solutions to life's tough problems instead of running away from the Army. If you are considering AWOL, DO NOT! It will only complicate your life further. Call your supervisor, First Sergeant, or the Commander for help.

Barracks Life Rules

- Do unto others, as you would have them do unto you.
- You break it, you pay for it.
- Clean up after yourself.
- Keep pornography out of public view.
- NO weapons.
- Keep it Locked and Secure.
- No matter how cool the music, if it can be heard outside your room, it's too loud.
- No smoking is allowed in the billets at any time, period.

Command Maintenance

Formation in the Motor pool every Monday. Leaders will be present during this time. Leaders are to check 5988s specifically to ensure parts from the last week are showing as ordered and spot check that all deficiencies are noted. All dispatches will be closed-out prior to last formation of the week.

Chaplain

Any Soldier can make an appointment at any time to see the Chaplain. Contact Chaplain at BN during duty hours, or XXX-XXXX, 24 hrs a day for the Duty Chaplain.

Complaint Procedures

Use the chain of command as the primary means to redress complaints within the unit. Soldiers have the right to register complaints directly with the Inspector General (IG). The IG channel exists for the benefit of all Soldiers and Soldiers must have confidence that they will not receive adverse action for using the IG channel.

Crime Prevention

If you own it, it is stolen on post, and there is no evidence that it had been secured, then YOU MAY NOT GET REIMBURSED for the loss. Therefore, keep your possessions locked up and, if valuable, out of sight. In the barracks, register items over $50 in value with the unit physical security NCO (or you cannot hope to be reimbursed for their theft). Unit can TEMPORARILY store high-dollar valuables in the supply room until you can secure them elsewhere. POC is (Supply). Ref: AR 735-5, ch 12.

Family Care Plans

If you have kids and are single or married to a service member, you will need a Family Care Packet. Operations will schedule an appointment with the Commander to complete this. The Commander will interview you and review the requirements for completing the packet. Once completed, ensure you keep the packet current as circumstances change, and return each year during your birth month to update your packet. POC is OPS. References are AR 600-20 (7 Jun 2006) and DA Pam 600-8 (Oct 1989).

Dining Facility Dress

You must wear Shoes and a Shirt for sanitation purposes. Your clothing must be in good repair and in good taste, reflecting your high status as a Soldier in the United States Army. I will not dictate the details of your wardrobe. If you are not sure what is meant by "Shoes", "Shirt", "Good Repair" or "Good Taste", ask your NCOIC.

Driving under the Influence / Abuse Prevention and Control

If you are under 21, you may not drink alcohol. If you drive a vehicle with a blood/alcohol content of .08% (.02% if under 21) or more, you are Driving While Intoxicated. Driving under the influence of alcohol or other drugs is dangerous, shows a lack of self-discipline, and is the quickest way to destroy your career. Do not Drive Drunk! If in doubt, call your supervisor.

We will have frequent urinalysis, selecting Soldiers at random to detect drug users. Get caught and you will receive punishment equal to the offense (usually a Field Grade Art 15), possible elimination from the Army, enrollment in ASAP, and possible loss of all earned military benefits. Soldiers who know they have a drug/alcohol problem are highly encouraged to ask for a referral to ASAP at no cost to their career.

Equal Opportunity

Soldier decisions and policies are based on the Soldier's performance, capability, fitness and merit; and NOT on the Soldier's race, color, national origin, age, religion or sex. Feel like you have been treated otherwise? Immediately use the chain of command, come straight to me, or call the EO NCO. Ref AR 600-20, chapter 6.

Leave/Pass

We usually have block leave in Dec and in the summer. Leave is still available at other times of the year; submit Leave and Pass Form 45 days out to have a better chance to get leave when requested. OCONUS leave requires a briefing/memo by the S2 shop to accompany the leave request. Do your homework and find the cheapest flights available 45 to 30 days out. Plane tickets usually go up significantly 14 days out from travel. Do not forget to ask if there is a military discount.

Physical Fitness

You should do PU & SU at least 3 days a week – outside of scheduled PT, start low and build every week. Concentrate on form and # reps without stopping. Score over 90 points in each event and qualify for the PT Patch.

Privately Owned Weapons (POWs)

All Soldiers living on post will register their POWs at the Provost Marshal; stop at the visitor's center first when coming on post. POWs are not allowed on post without proper registration and storage. Soldiers residing in the barracks will store their POWs in the arms room. Weapons, which are not firearms, will be stored in Supply. When transporting your POW: The weapon must be unloaded; the ammunition must be stored away from the weapon; and the weapon must not be within arm's reach. Ref: AR 190-11.

Redress of Grievances

If you have a problem with another Soldier, resolve it through the chain of command; if it involves the chain of command, use the open door policy. The Military version of the civilian lawsuit to recover damages is Article 138, UCMJ. See AR 27-10 for the format and guidance. The key is to act promptly, state the problem clearly and completely, and state specifically what action you desire taken.

Reenlistment Incentives

See the Career Counselor for current reenlistment incentives and available bonuses for reenlistment. College option of 6 months college attendance may be available. Ref: AR 601-80.

Safety

Safety First, Safety Always! Never take a shortcut when it comes to safety. Always wear the proper safety equipment, even if it is a "quick job." If you see a problem, do something to correct it. Leaders at all levels will conduct CRM prior to each training event.

Separate Rations

E6 and below, not residing with family, must have a Meal Card. Exceptions to this are based on Duty Requirements.

Sexual Harassment

Never treat members of the opposite sex in ways you would not like them to treat you...or your younger brother / sister. If YOU receive treatment you find sexually offensive, you must first tell the other person you do not like it. If they persist, it may be sexual harassment. I will not tolerate sexual harassment. Report violations promptly through the chain of command. Ref: AR 600-20

Sick Call Procedures

Get a sick call slip from your NCOIC and report to the Aid Facility at Squadron prior to going to Sick Call. If you acquire a profile, the doctor will give you a sick call slip with the profile information; bring a copy of it to the training room. Sick Call hours are:

Suicide Prevention

YOU are the first line of defense in identifying and helping someone considering suicide. Danger Signals: Soldier threatens suicide; Talks about wanting to die; Shows changes in behavior, appearance, mood; Abuses drugs or alcohol; Deliberately injures themselves; Appears depressed, sad, withdrawn. You can help: Remember "ACE" (Ask, Care, and Escort); Stay calm and listen; Let them talk about their feelings; be accepting; Do not judge; Ask if they have suicidal thoughts; Take threats seriously; do not swear secrecy; Stay with them; Tell Someone! Get Help, contact: 24 hr Suicide Hotline; 24hr Chaplain; Chain of Command; Supervisor; Mental Health; Emergency Operator (911); or go to the emergency room.

Possible Plan of Action:

- § Learning and perfecting assigned tasks
- § Learning about other section member's tasks
- § Learning about my leader's tasks
- § Enrolling in off-post civilian education and military correspondence courses
- § Improving APFT score
- § Achieving Expert Marksmanship on assigned weapon

- § Maintain good order and discipline
- § Setting an example on daily personal appearance and conduct on and off duty
- § Taking care of family
- § Being accountable
- § Being reliable
- § Provide the Soldier with a copy of the unit's METL and SOPs
- § Provide the Soldier with an outline of his/her job description and that of his peers and supervisor.
- § Assist the Soldier in enrolling in college classes and military correspondence courses
- § Provide the Soldier with a Career map of his MOS
- § Provide the Soldier with a copy of the promotion point worksheet and review it with him/her
- § Outline the standards for the Soldier of what you expect them to meet
- § Develop a plan to get your Soldier crossed trained within the Section/Squad/Team
- § Supervise the Soldier in performing all maintenance
- § Schedule the Soldier to administer physical training to his section/squad/team for a week.

Indebtedness

Possible Key Points for Discussion:

- Budget plan
- Over extended finances
- Root cause for the lateness on payments
- Failure to meet financial obligations could result in UCMJ
- Are creditors late receiving payments?

Possible Plan of Action:

SM

- § Attend the post budget counseling class 10 Aug 02
- § Make an appointment with the Unit Financial Advisor to get a budget drawn up within two weeks
- § Based on the budget, draft a plan to make payments to all creditors and provide a copy to the chain-of-command within three weeks

- § If over budgeted consider consolidating some of the bills
- § Stick with the budget until the financial problem has been resolved
- § Follow-up with the chain-of-command monthly until the financial problem is taken care of.

Leader

- § Enroll Soldier in the post budget counseling class. Schedule an appointment for the Soldier with the Unit Financial Advisor.
- § Review the budget plan.
- § Follow-up monthly to ensure the Soldier is staying within budget and all obligations are being paid.

DUI

Possible Key Points for Discussion:

- UCMJ
- General Letter of Reprimand
- On post driving restrictions
- Effects on military career
- Enrollment into the ASAP
- Any personal problems

Possible Plan of Action:

SM

- § Go to SJA for counseling and advice for receiving punishment under the UCMJ this week
- § Work to improve military bearing and appearance on and off duty by doing what is right
- § Today, arrange to have someone drop off and pick up from work while driving privileges are suspended
- § Enroll and attend all meetings at the ASAP
- § Do not consume alcohol
- § Seek counseling at ACS this week

Leader

- § Support the Soldier in overcoming hurdle
- § Get Soldier enrolled in ASAP
- § Schedule an appointment with SJA and ACS
- § Keep Soldier informed of all matters associated with the charges

Overweight

Possible Key Points for Discussion:

Age:
Ht:
WT
Auth WT:
BF:
Auth BF:

- Weight and tape standards IAW AR 600-9
- Authorized Weight and Height Table
- The impact on your career for failing the Army's weight standards
- Maintaining your leadership position
- Removal from the promotion standing list
- Bar to reenlistment
- Flagging actions placed on you and its impact
- Reenlistment
- Passes/Leaves
- Awards
- Placed in the Unit's Overweight Physical Fitness Program
- Medical screening
- Monthly weigh-ins

Possible Plan of Action:

SM

- § Become familiar with AR 600-9
- § Get enrolled in the unit's overweight physical fitness program
- § Attend the Nutrition class

- § Lose 3 to 5 pounds each month
- § Establish a physical fitness program for after duty hours
- § Use the advice from the Nutrition class for a diet and sticking with the diet
- § Weigh-in every two to three days to monitor weight loss
- § Inform the chain-of-command of any medical problems that may come up

Leader

- § Provide a copy of AR 600-9.
- § Enroll the Soldier in the unit's overweight program.
- § Flag Soldier for overweight.
- § Schedule the Soldier for a medical screening.
- § Schedule the Soldier for a Nutrition class.
- § Monitor the Soldier's progress and weigh Soldier every 30 days.
- § Do PT with the Soldier to give him/her moral support.

Pregnancy

Possible Key Points for Discussion:

- Retention or Separation
- Plans to stay in the Army after having child and make it a career
- Family Care Plan
- Profile
- Physical Fitness / Weight Control
- Leave:
- May go home to give birth
- Convalescent Leave
- Uniforms
- Housing
- Non-deployable status / Levy assignment
- Women, Infants, and Children (WIC) Program
- Problems

Possible Plan of Action:

SM

- § Start preparing a family care plan ASAP
- § Keep supervisor informed of all changes in profile and work only within the guidelines of the profile
- § Check with doctor to get an understanding of any restrictions the medications prescribed may have (driving, side effects)
- § Participate in the pregnancy Physical Fitness Program
- § Does not plan on going back home to deliver the baby, but will keep supervisor updated if this plan changes
- § Coordinate with the unit Supply Sergeant for maternity uniforms
- § Contact housing to get on the housing list
- § Enroll in the next financial budget class offered
- § Make an appointment with the WIC office to get information about the program and to get enrolled

Leader

- § Schedule appointment with the Company Commander for pregnancy counseling and initial Family Care Plan counseling.
- § Adjust duty hours/tasks in accordance with changes in profile.
- § Enroll her in the Pregnancy Physical Fitness Program.
- § Allow her time to visit ACS for financial planning, WIC, housing, and any other related matters.
- § Assist in any other issues that may develop.

Family Care Plan

Possible Key Points for Discussion:

It has come to my attention that you are currently a: (indicated by check mark)
    _____ Single parent
    _____ Member of a dual military couple
As a result, you are required to maintain a Family Care Plan. During this counseling session, I will inform you of the items you are required to maintain in your Family Care Plan. You will have 30 days from today's date to present your completed Family Care Plan to me. Failure to complete your Family Care Plan could result in a bar to reenlistment or separation from the military. Once your

Family Care Plan has been validated, you are required to update your Family Care Plan at a minimum:
- Once a year during your birth month
- If any changes occur that make your plan invalid
- As otherwise directed by the chain of command

You must also understand that the command may require you to execute your Family Care Plan for testing of validity (for example during exercises, alerts, and other unit activities). The command may periodically call your providers or guardians to ensure that they understand their responsibilities.

You are required to maintain the following forms in your Family Care Plan Packet:

1. _____DA Form 5304-R (Family Care Plan Counseling) (Signed by the Commander and Spouse's Commander when dual military)
2. _____DA Form 5305-R (Family Care Plan) (Approved by Commander/Spouse's Commander when dual military)
3. _____DA Form 5841-R (Special Power of Attorney for Guardianship) (Copy)
4. _____DA Form 5840-R (Certificate of Acceptance for Guardianship and Escort) (Original)
5. _____DD Form 1172 (ID Card Application – one per dependent)
6. _____DD Form 2558 (Allotment Form or other proof of financial support)
7. _____Letter of Instruction to Guardian(s) and Escort (Copy)
8. _____Will (Optional)

Possible Plan of Action:

- § Soldier stated that he/she understood the contents of the counseling. Soldier was directed to return to me no later than DATE for the final review and validation of the Family Care Plan. I also explained that should the Soldier need more time to complete the Family Care Plan they could request an extension in writing explaining why the extension is required.
- § For information purposes only: reviewed with the Soldier that failure to maintain a Family Care Plan could result in separation from the military. In addition, review requirements AR 635-200 Para 1-18(a) and notification of possible separation.
- § Request that Soldier list any areas that may currently be a problem:

Promotion

Possible Key Points for Discussion:

Requirements for PRIMARY Zone of Consideration:

Your Current Status:

- Study Material:
- Review question subject area checklist
- Read selected Army Regulations and Field Manuals
- Drill questions and answers
- Army Physical Fitness Test (APFT)
- Current score is
- Personal target score is 270+
- Weapon Qualification
- Current score is
- Personal target score is 40
- Chain of Command recommendation
- Mock Board
- Uniform inspection
- Check for proper fit
- Ensure all awards, tabs, and unit insignia are correct and up-to-date

Possible Plan of Action:

SM

- § Obtain a copy of the subject area checklist from PSG by Monday, Sept 16th.
- § Prepare and conduct a rigorous individual APFT program for 4 weeks
- § Take a record APFT on 9 October 02.
- § Go to unit range (September 23, 2002) to improve qualification score.
- § Practice D&C with the platoon for the next two weeks.
- § Build board appearance skills and control nervousness with Platoon mock board appearances each Thursday afternoon.
- § Provide supervisor with the necessary information to complete the recommendation packet by 27 Sep 02.
- § Bring in uniform on 27 Sep 02 so PSG can inspect it for proper fit and appearance.

§   Monitor all news reports at least the last two weeks prior to the board.
Leader

§   Assist with study progress by answering questions that may arise.
§   Schedule for an APFT with the Training NCO.
§   Inspect uniform prior to PSG's inspection.
§   Coordinate with Training NCO to add to the Range list
§   Coordinate with PSG for mock boards every Thursday until the date of the board.
§   Submit the recommendation packet through the chain-of-command to Battalion prior to the deadline.

Motorcycle Ownership

Possible Key Points for Discussion:

- Safety Rules and Enforcement
- Applicable References
- A Note to Leaders and Riders (Accident Awareness)
- Mandatory Training
- Relevant Directives and Regulations
- Installation Traffic Codes
- Analysis and Practice Notes (Potential actions to promote compliance with Motorcycle Safety Standards)
- Statement of Understanding
- Requirement Documents and Mandatory Personal Protective Equipment
- T-CLOCS Inspection Checklist

See Attached Commander's Motorcycle/ Recreational (ATV) Vehicle Operator Agreement.

Possible Plan of Action:

SM

§   Inform their CoC that they own or are planning to purchase a motorcycle.

- § Have Required Documents (Endorsement/ License, State Registration, Insurance and Post Registration) on-hand and up-to-date.
- § Attend and complete the appropriate Motorcycle Safety Foundation (BRC/ ERC2/ MSRC) Course, obtain and maintain their issued MSF card, and attend refresher training when required.
- § Wear all Mandatory Personal Protective Equipment EVERY time (On duty, off duty, On Post and Off Post) they operate a motorcycle.
- § Know all Applicable References and ensure that an NCO within their CoC conducts an updated T-CLOCS Inspection Checklist and a copy placed in the Motorcycle Safety Packet. (Completed Quarterly at the minimum)
- § Review, sign and complete all required administrative information (Statement of Understanding, Operator & Motorcycle Inspection Worksheet) within the Commander's Motorcycle/ Recreational (ATV) Operator Agreement.

Leader

- § Ensure all Motorcycle Riders received required counseling, review MC agreement and have SM sign and adhere to the terms.
- § Provide the time and opportunity for Soldier to attend the required training.
- § Monitor Soldier's ability to comply with all applicable rules and regulations.
- § Enforce Standards and Discipline.

WLC

Possible Key Points for Discussion:

- Review WLC checklist (Usually found on NCOA website)
- Review The Army School System (TASS) Unit Pre-Execution Checklist (TRADOC Form 350-18-2-R-E, Oct 2004)
- You may be expected to conduct an interview with the 1SG/CSM
- Work on giving PT, conducting drill and ceremonies, conduct basic land navigation course, review PMI, and practice conducting a class
- Inspect all equipment for serviceability and accountability
- DX unserviceable TA-50
- Ensure you have sufficient funds to defray the cost of:
  1. Haircuts

2. Laundry and Dry Cleaning
3. Personal Items (shaving gear, shoe polish, etc...)
- Ensure uniforms are in accordance with AR 670-1 (i.e. Proper Fit, Insignia, No Faded BDU's / ACU's, serviceable boots, etc.).
- Ensure that you have no appointments, pay problems, or personal problems, which will hinder you while attending this course.
- Know who your sponsor is and how to contact them. Ensure you have an alternate contact phone number.
- Review the following materials prior to course attendance:
  1. AR 670-1
  2. FM 21-20 or PRT
  3. FM 3-25.26 (Map Reading and Land Navigation)
  4. STP 21-1 SMCT (latest edition Common Task Manual Skill level 1)
  5. STP 21-24 SMCT (latest edition Common Task Manual Skill level 2)
- You must be able to meet the minimum Army standards on the APFT and body fat percentages during inprocessing. Height and weight will usually be measured on day one!
- Learn The Creed of the Noncommissioned Officer!
- Learn The Soldier's Creed!

Possible Plan of Action:

SM

- § Prepare to conduct PT once a week beginning next week
- § Prepare your class for my review
- § Continue to work on D&C
- § Ensure your equipment is prepared for my inspection on DATE
- § Conduct Diagnostic APFT on DATE
- § Obtain orders and meal card if required
- § Storage of POV and personal property plan was reviewed
- § Ensure all bills are paid in advance

Leader

- § Assist Soldier in preparing for all evaluation areas in WLC
- § Conduct diagnostic APFT
- § Schedule appointment with 1SG/CSM
- § Provide a sponsor for the Soldier

SSD

Possible Key Points for Discussion:

- On or about 25 May 2012, it was published from Squadron, from the United States Army Sergeants Major Academy:
- SUBJECT: ALARACT 288 / 2010 Structured Self Development (SSD) governance: Implementation of SSD policy
- SSD I. Effective 1 OCT 10 , Soldiers will be enrolled in SSD I automatically upon completing BCT / OSUT. Beginning FY 13,
- Soldiers must complete SSD I prior to attending WLC. Those Soldiers (PVT – SPC) who completed BCT / OSUT, but not WLC, prior to 1 Sep 10 will be automatically enrolled by 1 Jan 12 .
- THERE IS NO SSD BETWEEN WLC AND ALC.
- SSD III . Effective 1 May 11, all SGTs and SSGs who are graduates of ALC or BNCOC will be automatically enrolled in SSD III.
- SGTs (P), SSGs and SFCs will be enrolled in SSD III automatically upon completion of all phases of ALC.
- SSD IV. Effective 1 May 11, SSGs (P), SFCs, and MSGs will be enrolled automatically in to SSD IV upon completion of SLC.
- Effective 1 May 13, completion of SSD IV is a prerequisite for attendance to SMC.
- SSD V. Effective 1 May 11, MSGs (P) and SGMs will be enrolled automatically in to SSD V upon completion of Sergeant Major Course or its equivalent. Beginning 1 May 13, completion of SSD V is a prerequisite to be considered for nominative and joint assignments.

So with the above being said, all E-4s and E-4 promotable will complete SSD I before attendance to WLC. All E-5s that have not completed SSD I, will not attend WLC until complete and those that have WLC and have not completed SSD I, will not attend ALC or any other school and will not participate in any combat missions on Friday until complete. Those who do not complete SSD I will not attend a Soldier of the Month or Promotion Board and will potentially forfeit their promotable status. Again, failure to comply with this action is in violation of Article:
Article 92— Failure to obey order or regulation

Possible Plan of Action:

§ SM will make every effort to complete SSD and show progress IOT attend next level NCOES
§ Leader will monitor progress and provide duty time to accomplish SSD

Counseling Disciplinary Clause

Legal statement version #1

You are hereby notified that if this type of conduct continues, actions may be initiated under the Uniform Code of Military Justice to separate you from the Army prior to your scheduled ETS Date IAW AR 635-200. If you are involuntary separated, you could receive an Honorable Discharge, a General (Under Honorable Conditions) Discharge, or an Under Other Than Honorable Conditions Discharge. If you receive a discharge Under Other Than Honorable Conditions, you will be ineligible for reenlistment and for most benefits, including payments of accrued leave, transitional benefits, the Montgomery GI Bill, VA benefits, and you may face difficulty in obtaining civilian employment.

Legal statement version #2

Soldier was counseled concerning the performance and or conduct stated above and warned that future instances of poor performance or misconduct could result in recommendation for his separation from the service under Chapter 13, for Unsatisfactory Performance; Chapter 5-13 for Personality Disorder; Chapter 14 for Misconduct IAW AR 635-200. The Soldier was informed that because of separation under one of the chapters mentioned, he could receive a General or Other than Honorable (OTH) discharge certificate. The Solider was informed that if a General was issued he might lose certain benefits; or if an OTH discharge were approved, he would lose practically all benefits and could expect to encounter substantial difficulty in finding employment. He was informed that if he has less than two years active and reserve service at the time of discharge, he would be ineligible for VA benefits IAW Federal statute. The Soldier was told that if he was a contributor to the "New" GI Bill or the Army College Fund, and was separated before his ETS he would lose all his education benefits and forfeit all contributions he made to the fund. If discharged for either reason stated above, it would be nearly impossible to reenlist in any Armed Services in the future.

Finally, the Soldier was told that if a Less Than Honorable Discharge certificate was issued, he could make application to the Army Discharge Review Board and/or the Army Board for Correction of Military Records for upgrading; however, an act of consideration by either board would not imply that his discharge would actually be upgraded, as only a small percentage are.

Legal statement version #3

In addition to being counseled on the points above, he/she received counseling on the following: (1) That continued behavior similar to that for which he/she has been counseled may result in punishment under Article 15, UCMJ, court-martial, or adverse action such as a bar to reenlistment, suspension of favorable personnel actions (promotion, retention, school), or other appropriate administrative sanctions; (2) That if this behavior continues that separation under the provisions of AR 635-200 may be initiated; (3) That if separated prior to ETS, that he/she could receive either an honorable, general, or other than honorable discharge for their current term of service, or their term of service would be uncharacterized if they have served less than 180 days on active duty; (4) The basis for each characterization of service and the discharge certificates received for each and that his/her character of service would become part of a permanent record and may be provided to any Federal agency if they were to apply for either federal employment or security clearance; (5) The possible effects that each type of discharge would have on reenlistment, civilian employment, veteran's benefits, and related matters; (6) That a general discharge would cause loss of civil service retirement credit; (7) That an other than honorable discharge would result in him/her being reduced to the lowest enlisted rank, loss of payment of accrued leave, and loss of all benefits administered by the Veterans Administration and other federal and state agencies; (8) That separation prior to ETS may preclude him/her from enlisting in any component of the Armed Forces; (9) That separation prior to ETS may cause him/her to lose their entitlement to education benefits and money paid into the Army College Fund; (10) That separation prior to ETS may cause him/her to repay any unearned bonus received for enlistment or reenlistment; (11) That it would be unlikely that any attempt to have his/her characterization of service upgraded would be successful; (12) That he/she is encouraged to make every reasonable effort to ensure his/her performance and conduct meet military standards; (13) That he/she would be given a reasonable effort to bring their substandard performance and conduct to acceptable military standards.

Counseling Examples

AWOL

Event-Oriented:

Violation of article 86 (Absent without leave AWOL) of the Uniform Code Of Military Justice in that on or about 0630 26 April 2011 at Ft Bragg, NC you failed to report to your appointed place of duty, building C2 at the appointed time.

PVT Snuffy you are being counseled for AWOL (Absent without Leave) from 26 APRIL 2011 thru 29 APRIL 2011. On 26 APRIL 2011, we received two text messages from your phone stating that you were involved in an accident and that you had to go to the police station to file a report. After several unsuccessful attempts were made to contact you, we decided to call the police station to validate the text messages. The police had no knowledge of your whereabouts. We then called the local hospitals, and went to your home in an attempt to locate you. You could not be found. On the night of 29 APRIL 2011, the Commander was contacted by law enforcement stating they had you in custody at which point you were turned over to the Commander. The Commander then brought you to staff duty and explained that it was your place of duty until further notice. The next morning I arrived to question your motives and to determine if you were a "flight risk" meaning if you could be trusted not to go AWOL again. I then brought you to my office and read you your verbal rights and after you agreed to answer questions, I asked you what happened. You stated that you were blindfolded and abducted at gunpoint then brought to an unknown location and put in a closet to which you do not know how long you were there. You then stated that you were taken out of the closet days later and brought to the middle of some woods near Linden, NC and released in the middle of the night. You stated that you were dropped off at night and did not find anyone until the next evening at which point you found a fire station and reported what happened. After discussing the events and timelines that might explain your absents, you were ask to write a sworn statement. You refused and stated you wanted legal representation. At this time, I have determined that you are not a "flight risk" and have informed you of the importance of accountability. AWOL is a serious offense and will not go unnoticed; however, I have not made a decision on whether to recommend UCMJ and will investigate all possibilities and claims before proceeding. You will have an opportunity to speak with Trial Defense Services and I will consider your statements before making any decisions.

§ SM will inform Chain of Command on the status of the ongoing civilian investigation

§ SM will speak with Trial defense Services and notify the Chain of Command as to his decision to write a sworn statement

§ SM will continue with supervision to process out of the military under his current separation chapter

§ Leadership will exhaust all possible avenues and review all possible circumstances prior to making any decisions on UCMJ

Drug Related Incident

Event-Oriented:

Drug related incident

SPC Snuffy you were apprehended as a passenger in a vehicle that had open alcohol containers and drug paraphernalia to include open packs of SPICE and BATH SALTS. After being read your rights, you agreed, to answer questions. I asked you if you knew of the paraphernalia beforehand and you stated YES.____ I asked if you were in the vehicle and out at that time with the intentions of using these illegal substances and you stated NO.____ I feel that your answers were honest and forth coming, however, knowingly putting yourself in situations such as this can be detrimental to your carrier. I then asked if you ever used any of these illegal substances yourself and you stated YES.____ You stated that you experimented with SPICE in the past and asked if it was possible for self-enrollment into the ASAP program for further education and assistance with substance abuse. I stated I will support your self-enrollment in to ASAP but you will be given a command referral urinalysis for probable cause and if the results come back positive for illegal substances, you will be recommended for UCMJ. The use of illegal drugs jeopardizes your personal safety and the safety of those around you as well as the effectiveness of our unit to successfully accomplish the missions at hand and therefore will not be tolerated.

§ Leadership will ensure Soldier is afforded the opportunity for self-enrollment into the ASAP program

Marijuana

Event-Oriented:

Violation of article 112a (Wrongful use of controlled substances) of the Uniform Code Of Military Justice in that on 13 JAN 1947 you tested positive for THC after a unit wide urinalysis screening.

Wrongful use of marijuana is a crime and it is unacceptable behavior that will not be tolerated. Your test results from our unit urinalysis on 13 JAN 1947 came back positive for THC, a chemical found in marijuana. The maximum punishment for this offense is dishonorable discharge, forfeiture of all pay and allowances, and confinement for 2 years. Your reckless behavior jeopardized your personal safety and the safety of those around you as well as the effectiveness of our unit to successfully accomplish the missions at hand. (I am recommending UCMJ and maximum punishment for your misconduct.)

§ Leadership will ensure Soldier is present for all administrative, chapter and ASAP appointments.

Cocaine

Event-Oriented:

Violation of article 112a (Wrongful use of controlled substances) of the Uniform Code of Military Justice in that on 18 JUL 1947 you tested positive for COC (Cocaine) after a unit wide urinalysis screening.

Use of COCAINE is a crime and it is unacceptable behavior that will not be tolerated. This is your second offense. Test results from our unit urinalysis on 18 JUL 1947 came back positive for COC (Cocaine); side effects include a downward spiral of physical and mental deterioration. Cocaine smokers may suffer from severe respiratory problems like coughs, shortness of breath, severe chest pains, lung trauma, and bleeding. Because cocaine erodes away the membranes in the nose, nosebleeds are common in those individuals who snort cocaine. Some addicts permanently lose their sense of smell. There is no specific antidote for a cocaine overdose. Other long-term effects include: Violent behavior, confusion, mental illness that appears to be schizophrenia (paranoid feelings, picking at the skin, hallucinations); loss of appetite, which can result in severe weight loss; inability to sleep; increased heart and pulse rate, permanent damage to the blood vessels of the brain, which can lead to strokes, convulsions and body tremors, Chest pain and raised blood pressure, which can lead to a heart attack, Irregular heartbeat, and other negative impacts on your life. Your reckless behavior jeopardized your personal safety and the safety of those around you as well as the effectiveness of our unit to successfully accomplish the missions at hand. (I am recommending UCMJ with maximum punishment and immediate separation.)

§ Leadership will ensure Soldier is present for all administrative, chapter and ASAP appointments.

§ A separation physical, mental evaluation, and ACAP will be conducted as soon as possible.

Ecstasy and Amphetamine

Event-Oriented:

Violation of article 112a (Wrongful use of controlled substances) of the Uniform Code Of Military Justice in that on 18 JUL 1947 you tested positive for MDA LOL / MDMA (Ecstasy and Methylenedioxyamphetamine) after a Troop Level Urinalysis screening.

Wrongful use of MDA LOL / MDMA (Ecstasy and Methylenedioxyamphetamine) is a crime and it is unacceptable behavior that will not be tolerated. Your test results from a Troop Level Urinalysis on 18 JUL 1947 came back positive for MDA LOL / MDMA, chemicals found in Ecstasy and Methylenedioxyamphetamine. The maximum punishment for this offense is dishonorable discharge, forfeiture of all pay and allowances, and confinement for 2 years. Your reckless behavior jeopardized your personal safety and the safety of those around you as well as the effectiveness of our unit to successfully accomplish the missions at hand. Chapter for this offense begins immediately (I am recommending UCMJ for your misconduct.) You will also be command enrolled in to ASAP.

§ Leadership will ensure Soldier is present for all administrative, chapter and ASAP appointments.

§ A separation physical, mental evaluation, and ACAP will be conducted as soon as possible.

Lost ID Card

On or about 04 April 1947 SGT Snuffy, Joseph lost his Military Identification Card

SGT Snuffy, on 04 April 1947, you lost your Military Identification Card. Your Military ID card is government property. It is your responsibility to maintain your Military ID on your person at all times and report its loss or theft to the proper authorities immediately. Your negligent behavior has jeopardized the security of our military installations as well as military instillations around the world. You are required to report the loss of your Identification Card to the Provost Marshall and the ID card section of the PSB to have another Military Identification Card re-issued immediately.

§ Leadership will ensure SM understands the importance of accountability

§ SM will continue searching and provide feedback after seven calendar days as to the disposition of lost items

Jump Refusal

Event-Oriented:

Jump Refusal

SPC Snuffy you are being counseled for Jump Refusal as defined in the 82nd Airborne Division ASOP Edition VII (A paratrooper who has been to final manifest to green light and for some reason other than airsickness, physical impairment, aircraft equipment malfunction, or air item malfunction, voluntarily or willfully refuses to exit the aircraft.) Your equipment has been inspected in accordance with regulation and has been found serviceable. The jumpmaster and the safety reported that your jump refusal was due to a "panic attack" to which you stated you would not jump. In a time of need, this command has to have confidence that every Soldier will fulfill their duties without hesitation. I have lost the confidence that you can successfully perform your duties as a paratrooper in the 82nd Airborne Division. I am recommending that the Commander impose non-judicial punishment for your inability to perform your duties. Furthermore, I am recommending reassignment for you to a non-airborne unit. IAW AR 600-8-22 Military Awards section (1–31) paragraph (2) Parachutist Badge. Any Parachutist badge may be revoked when the awardee is punished under the Uniform Code of Military Justice (UCMJ) for refusal to participate in a parachute jump. It is not my recommendation that your badge be revoked; however, it is the Commander's decision. "AIRBORNE!"

§ Leadership will ensure Soldier is informed and understands the consequences of his actions.

Speeding

Event-Oriented:

For speeding, reckless driving, and running stop signs

SPC SNUFFY you are being counseled for speeding, reckless driving, and running stop signs. The Commander witnessed you driving through the parking lot this morning at approximately 1030 hrs, he said you were speeding while driving through the parking lot, then, when exiting you failed to stop. He also witnessed you run the stop sign. This is in violation of on post regulations and local and national law. If this type of disregard for the law and the safety of yourself and others continues, your on post driving privileges can be revoked. You will also be subject to UCMJ. See back for corrective action.

§ SM will write a 500-word essay on motorcycle vehicle safety

§ SM will prepare a 30-minute slide based safety class on motorcycle safety to be briefed to the entire troop

§ SM will attend the next on post-defensive driver's class at the Soldier Readiness Center starting 0700 Saturday mornings and then provide a copy of the certificate to the 1SG

Jump Master Proficiency

Informative counseling – Jump Master Proficiency requirements

You are being counseled on Jump Master Proficiencies. As a leader in the 82nd Airborne Division, you will make every attempt to attain a "White Slip" from the Advanced Airborne School (AAS) then attend and graduate Advanced Airborne School. Jumpmasters are an integral part of the BCT, they are required to ensure the success of Airborne Operations and they provide the ability to execute the Squadron's Mission Essential Tasks. Above all other aspects as a LEADER in the 82nd Airborne Division you are always expected to know more be more and do more than your Soldiers do. The effective deployment and utilization of airborne forces requires Leaders at all levels to be knowledgeable and proficient in tasks that Paratroopers are not expected to know. The success of this training is imperative because Leaders are looked upon differently by their Soldiers in the 82nd Airborne Division Soldiers will follow out of trust and willfully execute any and all directives. The study material and all of the equipment necessary for you to be successful will be or has been provided by this organization, if you feel like you are short on knowledge or equipment there are study groups throughout the week based on the necessity of tasking. This is such an important facet of our organization that the squadron even has study groups based on the availability of Jumpmasters. If you want something bad enough you will find time outside of your work, you will put forth maximum effort, and you will be successful. You are an important member of the team because of the leadership position that you fill. Personnel who want to attend the Jumpmaster course: must have 12 static line jumps from U.S. Air Force aircraft (this may be waived by the 82nd Airborne Division Chief of Staff for personnel that are taking command), 12 months on jump status, and 12 months retain ability.

• Required equipment for Pre-Test:

ID tags, ID card, Harness Single Point Release, Hook Pile Tape Lowering Line, ALICE pack with frame (outer accessory pouches filled and weighing 35lbs.).

• Required equipment for jumpmaster course:

1. Report time is 0600 hrs for primary slot holders and they must possess a current Pre-Test slip (dated within 90 days of the course start date and has a RED USA AAS stamp), Valid ID card, and ID tags. Primary slot holders must have a memorandum IAW the Corps and DIV G-3 schools guidance and a copy of their Jump Log (DA Form 1307). CPLs will also require an additional memorandum signed by their first O-6 in their chain of command or Commander for separate companies.

2. Students that are attending the course are required to have the following: serviceable ACUs, serviceable boots (no civilian footgear or shoelaces constructed of Type II/III nylon cord), ID card, ID tags, tan/brown t-shirt (no unit t-shirts), beret (no rigger hats or patrol caps), 2qt. canteen or other hydration apparatus, ALICE pack/MOLLE with frame weighing 35 lbs. or more, maps (Ft. Bragg East/ West and Camp Mackall), protractor, Advanced Combat Helmet without the camouflage cover (all component parts must be serviceable).

§ Leadership will reinforce study times and equipment availability for Jump Master "white slip".

§ SM will state desire, if any, to achieve "White Slip", then Jump Master School, and outline a course of action to achieve these goals.

Insubordination

Event-Oriented:

Insubordination

SFC Snuffy, you are being informed that I am relieving you of your additional duties as Platoon Sergeant. I am not satisfied with your performance. On several occasions, I have verbally counseled you for disrespecting Soldiers unnecessarily, for being indiscreet with Soldier's personal issues, for expressing your personal negative views towards the senior leadership in front of Soldiers, for going directly to officers without my knowledge stating dissatisfaction with my decisions, and for making rhetorical comments when advised on your Leadership style. Other officers and senior leaders in this company expressing their concerns with the amount of undue stress you put on your Soldiers have also approached me. These actions undermine my authority; it also breeds resentment, stifles initiative, and lowers morale among your Soldiers. I have to be able to trust you and you have to be able to trust my decisions or address them with me personally. As a Platoon Sergeant, I consider you my direct link to the Soldiers and therefore expect you to share my views toward certain issues such as our Leaderships desire for senior leaders to attain white slip and Jump Master School. You have stated several times that you have no intention of going to the Jump Master course and never having attained white slip is a testament to that. Your behavior is counterproductive and these poor leadership traits will no longer be tolerated. All of my expectations are still the same. I expect you to provide purpose, direction AND motivation for your Soldiers. I expect you to do a proper and satisfactory handover with your replacement, and if the Platoon Sergeant deems it necessary to leave you in charge in his absence, I expect you to perform those acting Platoon Sergeant duties considering this counseling. If you are having trouble adjusting to my expectations, address the issue with me personally and I will explain it in further detail. As a senior NCO, you will be professional and continue to perform your duties as deemed by your MOS. This is not a Relief for Cause nor will you receive a change of rater as your duty position remains the same, however, this incident will be annotated under Leadership on your next evaluation report.

§ You will fully brief your replacement on Soldiers issues and do a proper handover

§ You will be reevaluated by the First Sergeant after a 30-day period

Extra Duty and Restriction

PVT Snuffy was counseled on his requirements for extra duty:

1. Number of days Extra duty: 14

2. Number of days Restricted: 14

3. Beginning date: Ending date:

o Uniform is ACUs (SQDN SDNCO may change the uniform requirements if task requires it).

o Report times for extra duty: Weekdays Extra duty is from 1800 until mission complete or No Earlier Than 2300. Saturdays, Training Holidays, Holidays report times are 0900-2300. Sundays report times are 1300-2300. Extra duty personnel will be released when all tasks are completed but NET 2300, (All release times are based on the SDNCO requirements to ensure mission/task are completed).

o Meals: Extra duty personnel are required to eat prior to reporting for duty. For meals that fall during scheduled work period, extra duty personnel are allowed 30 minutes for meals. All meals must be consumed either in the closest open dinning facility or in the Squadron Headquarters/Troop Command Post.

o Extra duty personnel are not authorized outgoing phone calls or visitors unless it's an emergency.

o Soldier was counseled on his responsibility to perform his extra duty, to report at the designated times in the proper uniform and that only the 1SG is authorized to excuse him from extra duty.

o Restriction: Soldier was informed his restriction will be handled at Troop level and that he is restricted to the Brigade area for the time period stated above. The Brigade Area includes the following places: Squadron Headquarters, Troop Command Posts, DFAC, and Squadron Motor Pool (Soldier must sign out with their unit CQ to go to their place of worship and PX for essential items only with NCO escort approved by his 1SG).

Example Memorandum

Recommendation for Future Employment

MEMORANDUM FOR RECORD

SUBJECT: Professional Assessment for Future Employment

PURPOSE: To provide performance based insight on John T. Snuffy from JUN 2009 through JUN 2013

1.   It is my professional opinion that during this time John T. Snuffy showed tremendous character, diversity and a willingness to do what was necessary to accomplish the task at hand. Not only was he able to identify critical points during problem solving but also his foresight and attention to detail allowed him to resolve issues before they became problematic. It was his high spirited and optimistic attitude that motivated others to be the best. John's interpersonal and communication skills were essential in building foreign relationships that greatly benefited our government. He was always punctual, informative and excited about work. His posture and ability to articulate during conversation demonstrated confidence that was necessary in our demanding work environment. As a leader John was able to instill loyalty and provide guidance through example, this set him apart from his peers and truly warrants recognition.

2.   I recommend John T. Snuffy be placed in positions of great responsibility whenever possible. I have no doubt he will become a valued asset to any organization.

POINT OF CONTACT:

Flow Charts

Recurring Task:

4833 Processing

UCFR

Inventories

- Monthly Hand Receipt
- Sensitive Items

PAI Procedures

GPC Card

Urinalysis

Schools

Counseling

Event Driven:

AWOL

DFR

AWOL / DFR Clothing inv.

Suicide Ideation / Attempt

Positive UA

DUI

Domestic Abuse

Lautenberg Amendment

Sexual Harassment

Sexual Assault

WTB Nomination

Hospitalization

Family Care Plan

Suspense of Favorable Actions

Bar to Reenlistment

FLIPL

Soldier Death

EFMP

Health and Welfare Inspections

Off Post Apprehension / Confinement

Advancement Wavers

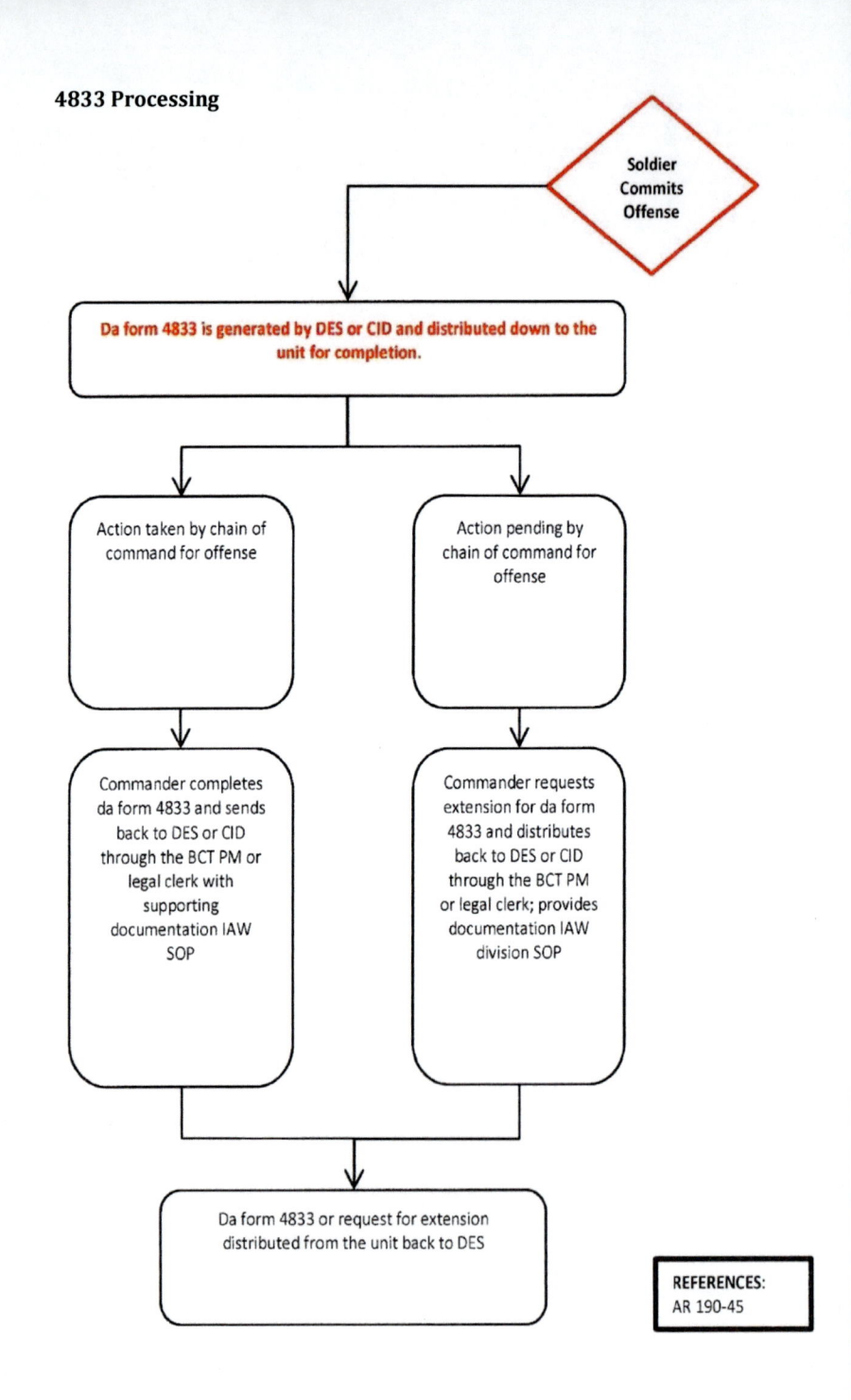

4833 Processing

```
                                            ┌─────────────┐
                                            │   Soldier   │
                                            │   Commits   │
                                            │   Offense   │
                                            └─────────────┘
                                                   │
                                                   ▼
          ┌──────────────────────────────────────────────────┐
          │ Da form 4833 is generated by DES or CID and       │
          │ distributed down to the unit for completion.      │
          └──────────────────────────────────────────────────┘
                    │                               │
                    ▼                               ▼
         ┌────────────────────┐         ┌────────────────────┐
         │ Action taken by    │         │ Action pending by  │
         │ chain of command   │         │ chain of command   │
         │ for offense        │         │ for offense        │
         └────────────────────┘         └────────────────────┘
                    │                               │
                    ▼                               ▼
         ┌────────────────────┐         ┌────────────────────┐
         │ Commander completes│         │ Commander requests │
         │ da form 4833 and   │         │ extension for da   │
         │ sends back to DES  │         │ form 4833 and      │
         │ or CID through the │         │ distributes back to│
         │ BCT PM or legal    │         │ DES or CID through │
         │ clerk with         │         │ the BCT PM or legal│
         │ supporting         │         │ clerk; provides    │
         │ documentation IAW  │         │ documentation IAW  │
         │ SOP                │         │ division SOP       │
         └────────────────────┘         └────────────────────┘
                    │                               │
                    └───────────────┬───────────────┘
                                    ▼
                 ┌──────────────────────────────────────┐
                 │ Da form 4833 or request for extension│
                 │ distributed from the unit back to DES│
                 └──────────────────────────────────────┘
```

REFERENCES:
AR 190-45

UCFR

EVENT START

- Battalion S-1 receives UCFR from Brigade S-1.

- Company receives UCFR from Battalion S-1.

- Check to ensure all Soldiers are listed on the UCFR; if not:
  - Provide 1 copy of all supporting documents (i.e. PCS, Intra-Post Transfer, ETS, and Retirement orders) to add or delete the Soldier.

- Check to ensure Soldiers data (i.e. BAQ/BAS, leave balance, pay grade) are accurate according to the displayed criteria; if not:
  - Provide 1 copy of all supporting documentation (i.e. promotion orders, DA 31, Article 15 Forfeitures).

- Check to ensure last month's corrections were made; if not:
  - Attach copies of previous UCFR to current. Annotate all changes needed.

- Once the company level review has been completed:
  - Company Commander will sign the UCFR.
  - Company will make a copy for their internal files.
  - Company will return UCFR to Battalion S1 with all supporting documents NLT the designated suspense date.

- Battalion S-1 receives completed UCFR from company, ensuring all documents are provided

- Brigade S-1 receives completed UCFR from Battalion S-1

- UCFR must be submitted to Finance by the 10th of the month

REFERENCES:
AR 600-8-6
DoD FMR 7A

FLOW CHARTS

Monthly Hand Receipt

```
                                                    ┌─────────────┐
                                                    │   Monthly   │
                                                    │  Inventory  │
                                                    └─────────────┘
                                                           │
┌──────────┐   ┌──────────┐   ┌──────────┐    ┌──────────┐
│   PBO    │   │ Co Cdr   │   │ Conduct  │    │ Property │
│identifies│──▶│ notifies │──▶│   10%    │───▶│ On-Hand? │
│ 10% PB   │   │ sub-HR   │   │ Monthly  │    └──────────┘
│   ...    │   │ holders  │   │Inventory │     Yes │  │ No
└──────────┘   └──────────┘   └──────────┘         │  │
                                                   ▼  ▼
```

Flow (in reading order):

- Monthly Inventory →
- PBO identifies 10% PB to be inventoried for month →
- Co Cdr notifies sub-HR holders when & how inventory is to be conducted →
- Conduct 10% Monthly Inventory →
- **Property On-Hand?**
  - **No** → Initiate FLIPL
  - **Yes** → Check property condition →
    - **Property Damaged ???**
      - **Yes** → Report damage to Maintenance
      - **No** → Check end-Items for completeness using TM or SC →
        - **Component shortages?**
          - **Yes** → Make List of shortages → Report to PBO
          - **No** → Check serial # on item if applicable →
            - **Difference in serial #?**
              - **Yes** → Report to PBO
              - **No** → Complete Inventory of all LINs mandated → Record the results/adjustments on HR with PBO → Sign HR at PBO

REFERENCES:
AR 735-5

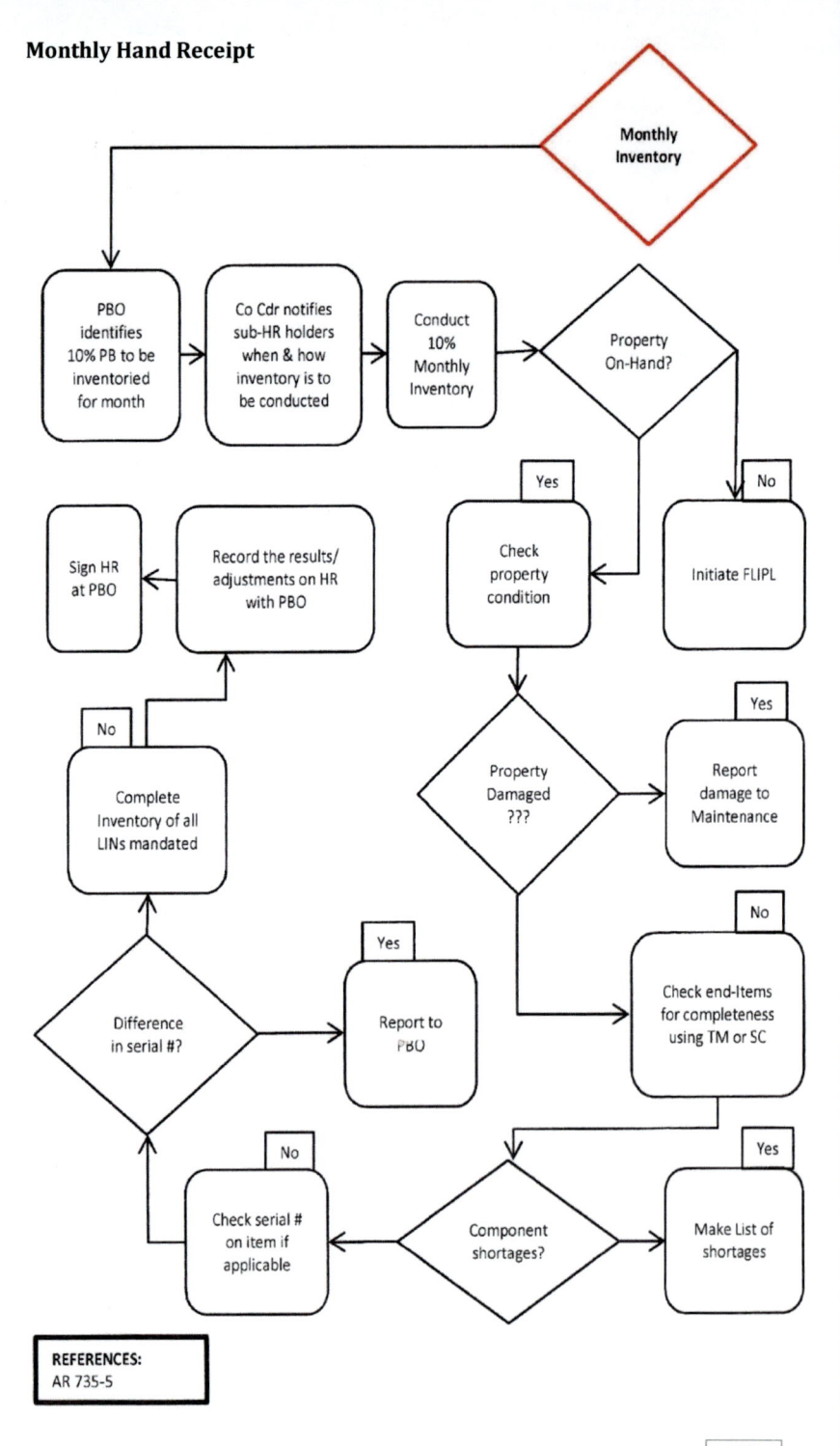

Sensitive Items Inventory

```
                                              ┌─────────────┐
                                              │ Sensitive   │
                                              │ Items (SI)  │
                                              │ Inventories │
                                              └─────────────┘
                                                    │
         ┌──────────────────────┬───────────────────┤
         ▼                      ▼                   ▼
┌─────────────────┐   ┌─────────────────┐   ┌─────────────────┐
│ PBO identifies  │   │ Co Cdr notifies │   │ SFC (+) conduct │
│ 100% Sensitive  │──▶│ sub-HR holders  │──▶│ SI Monthly      │
│ Items to be     │   │ when & how      │   │ Inventory.      │
│ inventoried for │   │ inventory is to │   │ Cannot inspect  │
│ month           │   │ be conducted    │   │ two consecutive │
│                 │   │                 │   │ months          │
└─────────────────┘   └─────────────────┘   └─────────────────┘
```

Decision flow:

- **Property On-Hand?**
  - **Yes** → Check property condition
  - **No** → Report SIR/Initiate 15-6 Investigation/FLIPL

- **Property Damaged ???**
  - **Yes** → Report damage to Maintenance
  - **No** → Check end-Items for completeness using TM or SC

- **Component shortages?**
  - **Yes** → Make List of shortages → Check serial # on item if applicable
  - **No** → Check serial # on item if applicable

- **Difference in Serial #?**
  - **Yes** → Report to PBO
  - **No** → Complete Inventory of all LINs mandated → Record the results/adjustments on HR with PBO → Sign HR at PBO

REFERENCES: AR 735-5

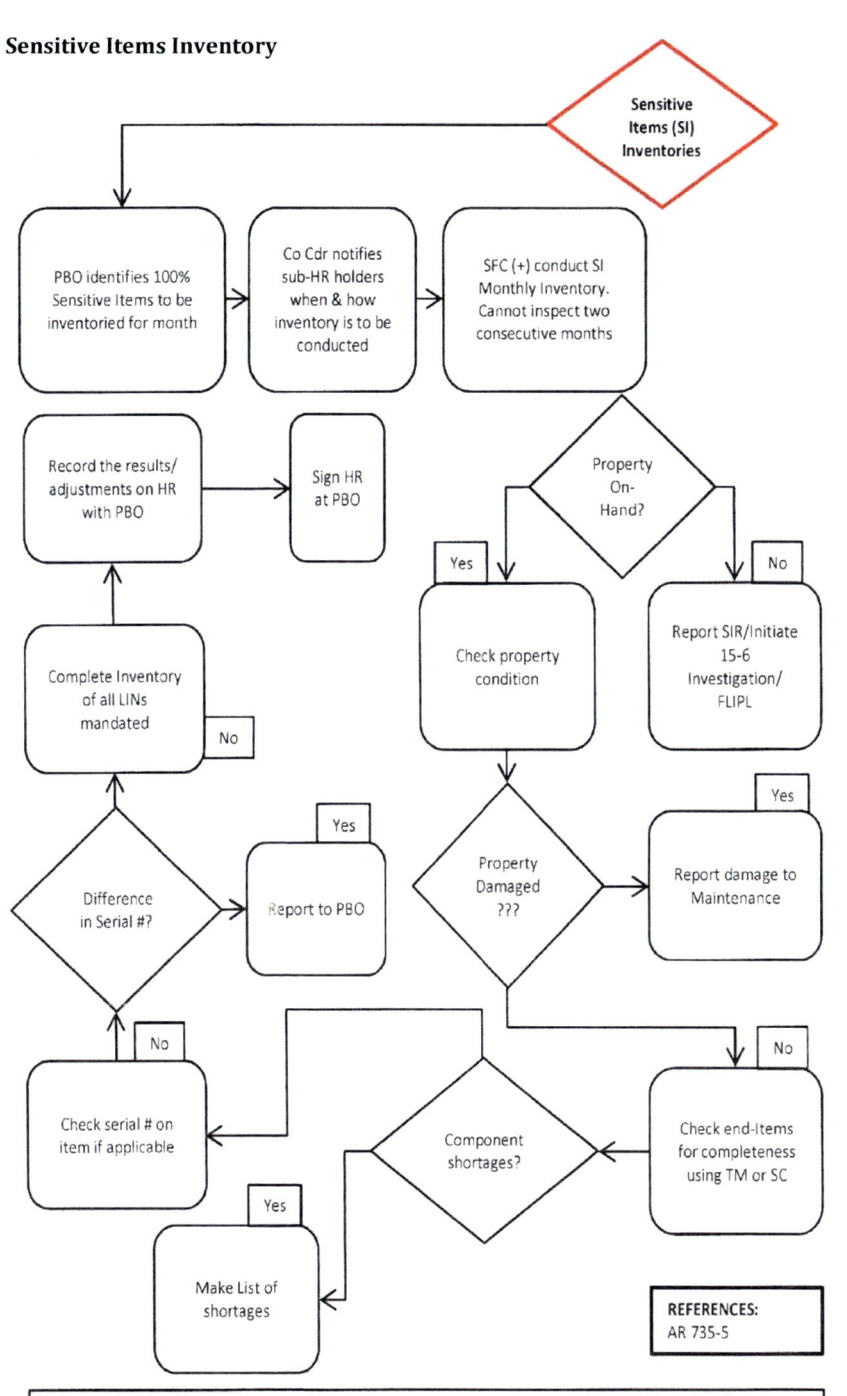

Although commanders may designate a person to conduct the sensitive items inventories, it is strongly encouraged that commanders be present during the inventories.

PAI Procedures

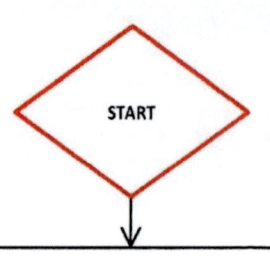

```
START
```

Determine whether a PAI is required:
- HRC directed.
- Change of Command.
- Reconciliation of personnel databases (i.e. EMILPO).

Prior to PAI CDR / 1SG review the AAA-162 to ensure all Soldier's data (name, rank, SSN) are accurate, if not:
- Provide 1 copy of all supporting document (promotion orders) to rectify the discrepancy to BN S1.

Conduct the PAI using corrected AAA-162.
If Soldier present for duty:
- Verify that Soldier's CAC Card and ID Tags are current and accurate. Soldier ensures all personal data fields on the AAA-162 is correct and then initials by their name.

If Soldier is not present for duty:
- Provide supporting documentation for Soldiers not present (DA 31, DD 1610, quarters slip). Though documentation meets requirements of PAI, recommend telephonic contact for all those not present.

Once the PAI has been completed:
- Company Commander will sign the AAA-162 and DA 3986.
- Company will maintain a copy of the PAI packet in the proper filing system and forward the original copies to the BN S1.

REFERENCES:
AR 600-8-6
AR 600-8-104
AR 600-8-105
FM 1.0
AAA-162
DA 3986

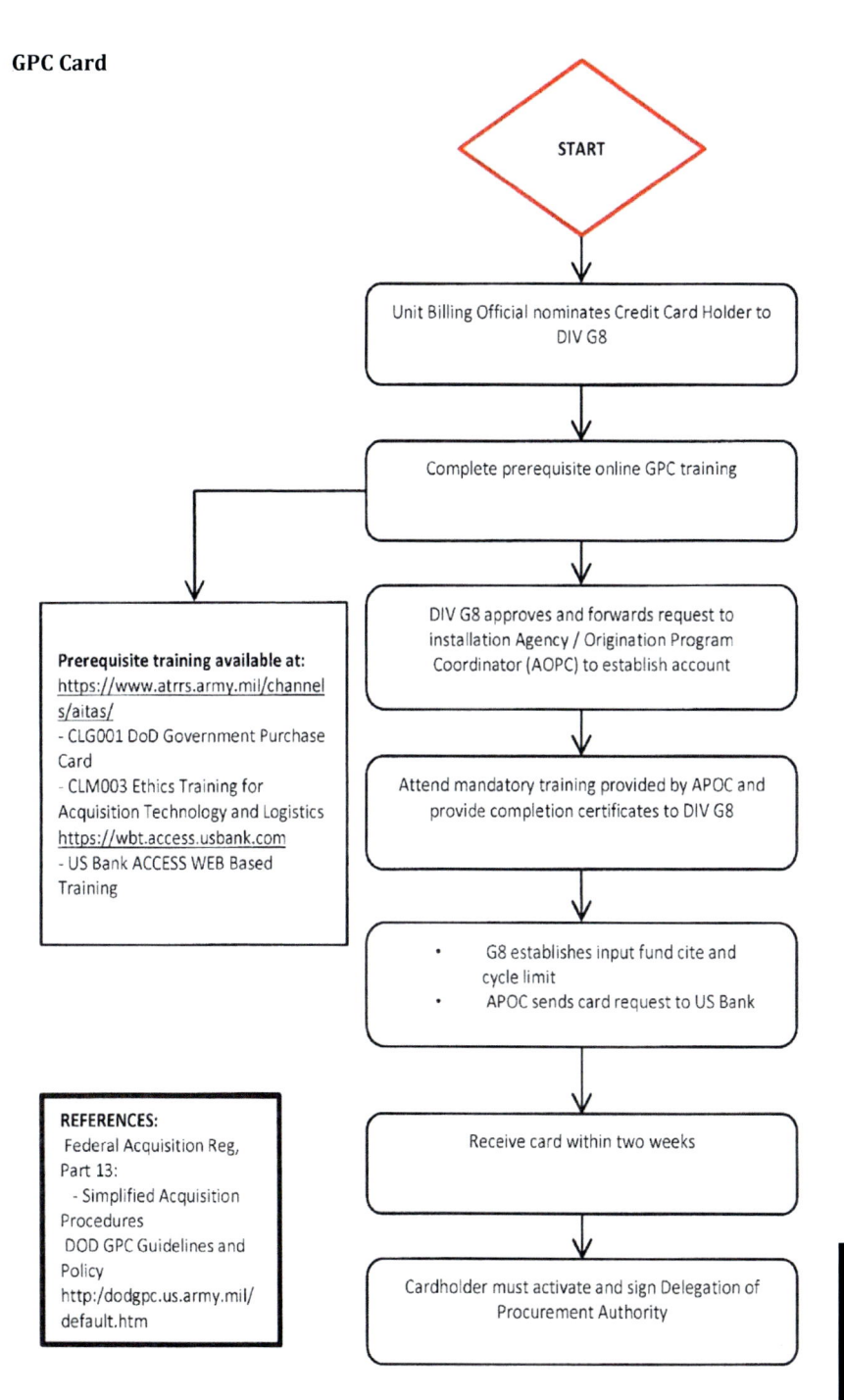

GPC Card

```
                          START
                            │
                            ▼
         ┌──────────────────────────────────────┐
         │ Unit Billing Official nominates      │
         │ Credit Card Holder to DIV G8         │
         └──────────────────────────────────────┘
                            │
                            ▼
         ┌──────────────────────────────────────┐
    ┌───▶│ Complete prerequisite online GPC     │
    │    │ training                             │
    │    └──────────────────────────────────────┘
    │                       │
    │                       ▼
    │    ┌──────────────────────────────────────┐
    │    │ DIV G8 approves and forwards request │
    │    │ to installation Agency / Origination │
    │    │ Program Coordinator (AOPC) to        │
    │    │ establish account                    │
    │    └──────────────────────────────────────┘
    │                       │
    │                       ▼
    │    ┌──────────────────────────────────────┐
    │    │ Attend mandatory training provided   │
    │    │ by APOC and provide completion       │
    │    │ certificates to DIV G8               │
    │    └──────────────────────────────────────┘
    │                       │
    │                       ▼
    │    ┌──────────────────────────────────────┐
    │    │ • G8 establishes input fund cite and │
    │    │   cycle limit                        │
    │    │ • APOC sends card request to US Bank │
    │    └──────────────────────────────────────┘
    │                       │
    │                       ▼
    │    ┌──────────────────────────────────────┐
    │    │ Receive card within two weeks        │
    │    └──────────────────────────────────────┘
    │                       │
    │                       ▼
    │    ┌──────────────────────────────────────┐
    │    │ Cardholder must activate and sign    │
    │    │ Delegation of Procurement Authority  │
    │    └──────────────────────────────────────┘
```

Prerequisite training available at:
https://www.atrrs.army.mil/channels/aitas/
- CLG001 DoD Government Purchase Card
- CLM003 Ethics Training for Acquisition Technology and Logistics
https://wbt.access.usbank.com
- US Bank ACCESS WEB Based Training

REFERENCES:
Federal Acquisition Reg, Part 13:
 - Simplified Acquisition Procedures
DOD GPC Guidelines and Policy
http:/dodgpc.us.army.mil/default.htm

Urinalysis

```
        ┌─────────────┐
        │   Conduct   │
        │  Urinalysis │
        └─────────────┘
```

Commander determines when a 100% urinalysis will be conducted for the company

Commander is provided the date / time to conduct their portion of the 4% weekly random urinalysis as determined by the Battalion Prevention Leader.

↓

Commander monitors the proper implementation and process of the urinalysis program; ensures that there is a NCO (E-5 or above) assigned as the Primary Unit Prevention Leader and Alternate Unit Prevention Leader and those personnel have attended training IAW AR 600-85, paragraph 9-6.

↓

Urinalysis Program Requirements

- Document that all newly assigned Soldiers are briefed on ASAP policies and services within 30 days of arrival.

- Commander monitors the Primary / Alternate UPL to ensure positive chain of custody is maintained with samples provided; this reduces the number of voided samples that will not be processed at the laboratory.

- Maintain ASAP elements while deployed, to the maximum extent possible (see Para 4–7 of AR 600-85 for details.)

- Implement ASAP prevention and education initiatives addressed in chapter 9 AR 600-85. Ensure that all Soldiers receive a minimum of 4 hours of alcohol and other drug abuse training per year in accordance with TRADOC Reg 350–70.

REFERENCES:
AR 600-85
TRADOC Reg 350-70

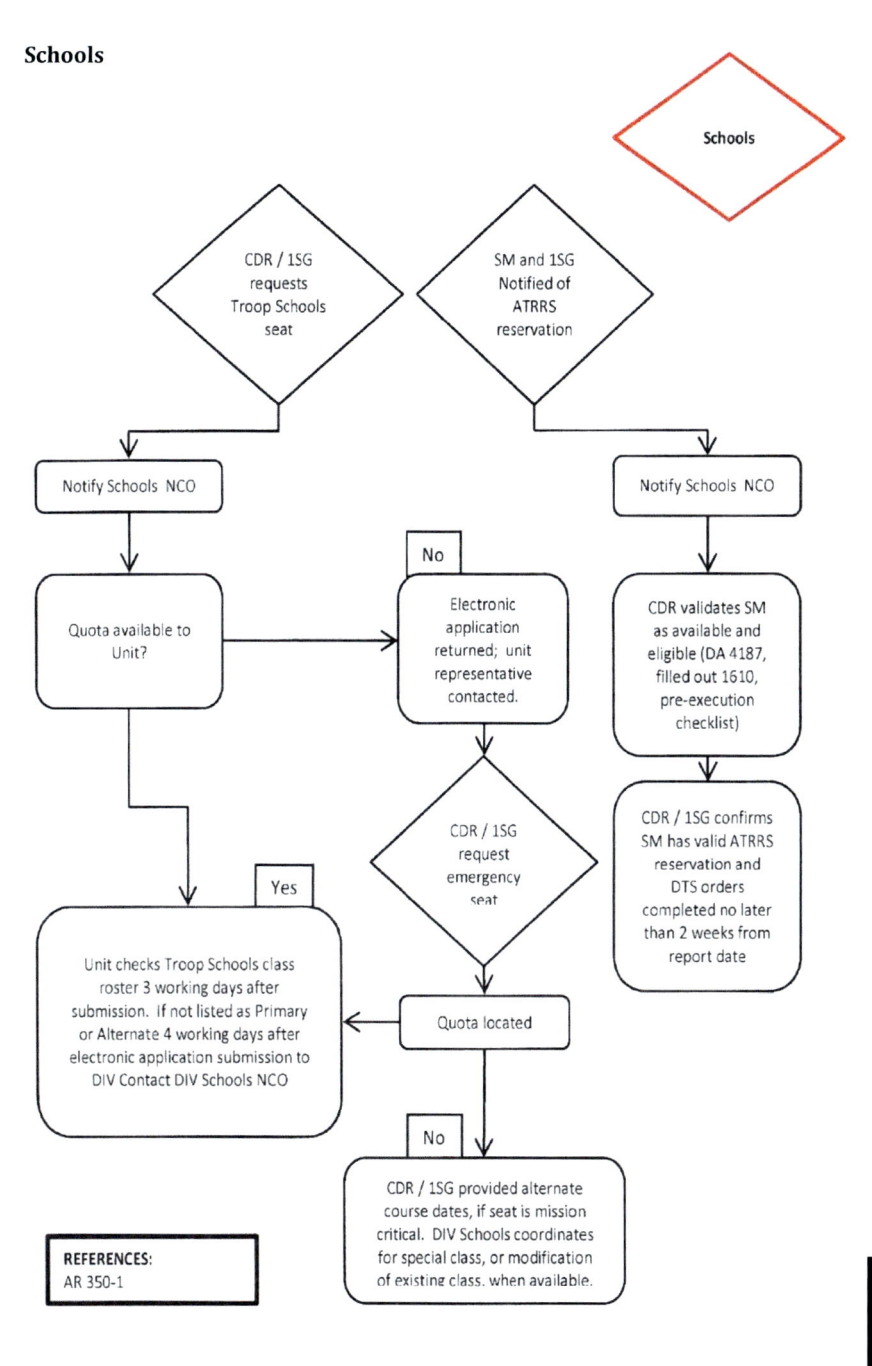

Schools

```
                                                          ◇ Schools ◇

        ◇ CDR / 1SG              ◇ SM and 1SG
          requests                 Notified of
          Troop Schools            ATRRS
          seat ◇                   reservation ◇

        Notify Schools NCO       Notify Schools NCO

        [Quota available to]     [Electronic              [CDR validates SM
         Unit?                    application              as available and
                          ──No──▶ returned; unit           eligible (DA 4187,
                                  representative           filled out 1610,
                                  contacted.]              pre-execution
                                                           checklist)]

                                                          [CDR / 1SG confirms
                                 ◇ CDR / 1SG               SM has valid ATRRS
                          ─Yes─▶   request                 reservation and
                                   emergency               DTS orders
                                   seat ◇                  completed no later
                                                           than 2 weeks from
        [Unit checks Troop Schools class                   report date]
         roster 3 working days after
         submission. If not listed as Primary
         or Alternate 4 working days after   ◀── [Quota located]
         electronic application submission to
         DIV Contact DIV Schools NCO]
                                                  │
                                                  No
                                                  ▼
                                      [CDR / 1SG provided alternate
                                       course dates, if seat is mission
        REFERENCES:                    critical. DIV Schools coordinates
        AR 350-1                       for special class, or modification
                                       of existing class, when available.]
```

FLOW CHARTS

Counseling

```
                    ┌─────────────┐
                    │ EVENT START │
                    └─────────────┘
                           │
            ┌──────────────┴──────────────┐
            ▼                             ▼
   ┌──────────────────┐         ┌──────────────────┐
   │    E4 & Below    │         │    E5 & above    │
   │ Monthly Counseling│        │Quarterly Counseling│
   └──────────────────┘         └──────────────────┘
```

E4 & Below — Monthly Counseling

1SG will review and check that counseling (monthly, negative, positive) are being conducted according to standards. Use DA Form 4856 for monthly counseling.

↓

Include in counseling specific situational counseling such as APFT, Height / Weight failure, High Risk Soldier behavior, and Soldiers eligible for promotion but not recommended. Use rehabilitative portion of DA 4856

↓

1SG ensures leader and Soldier actions identified during counseling are being conducted.

↓

Monitor performance; evaluate progress

E5 & above — Quarterly Counseling

CDR / 1SG will verify rater is conducting quarterly counseling. Use DA Form 2166-8-1 for initial counseling and quarterly counseling. *Officers counseled on 67-9-1*

↓

Include specific situational counseling such as APFT, Height / Weight failure, High Risk Soldier behavior, and Soldiers eligible for promotion but not recommended.

↓

CDR / 1SG ensure leader and Soldier actions identified during counseling are being conducted.

↓

Monitor performance; evaluate progress.

REFERENCES:
AR 623-3
AR 635-200
DA PAM 623-3
FM 22-100

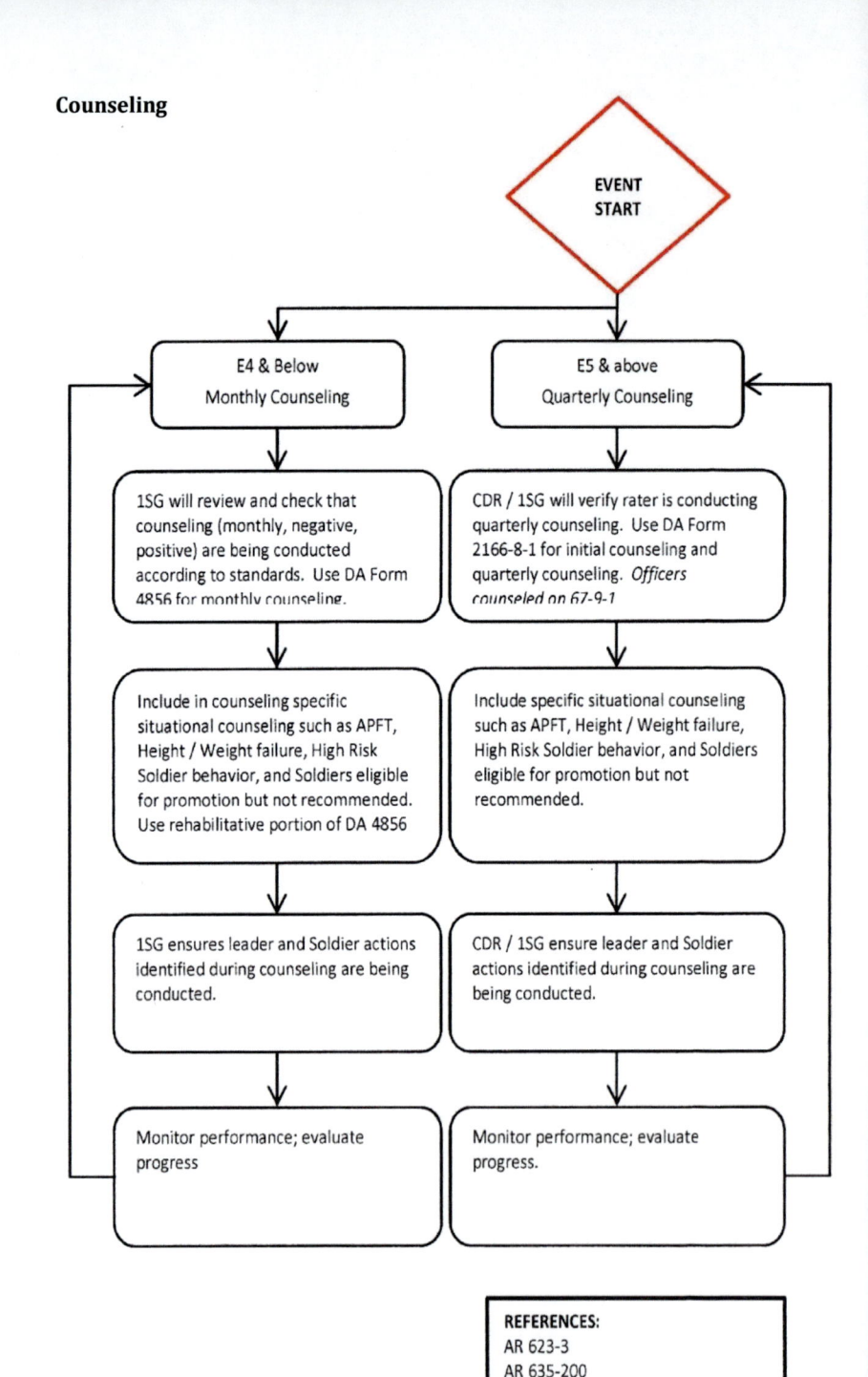

AWOL

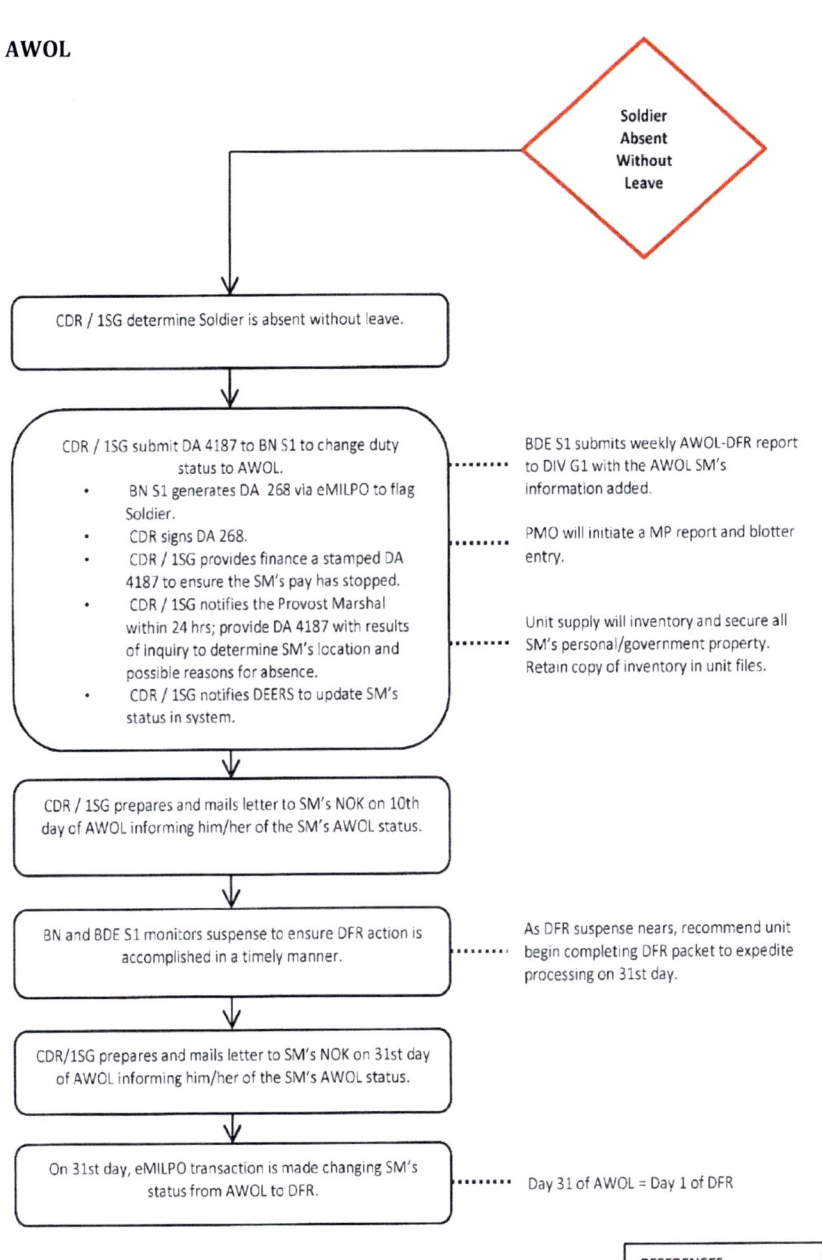

```
                              ┌─────────────┐
                              │   Soldier   │
                              │   Absent    │
                              │  Without    │
                              │   Leave     │
                              └──────┬──────┘
                                     ▼
```

CDR / 1SG determine Soldier is absent without leave.

CDR / 1SG submit DA 4187 to BN S1 to change duty status to AWOL.
- BN S1 generates DA 268 via eMILPO to flag Soldier.
- CDR signs DA 268.
- CDR / 1SG provides finance a stamped DA 4187 to ensure the SM's pay has stopped.
- CDR / 1SG notifies the Provost Marshal within 24 hrs; provide DA 4187 with results of inquiry to determine SM's location and possible reasons for absence.
- CDR / 1SG notifies DEERS to update SM's status in system.

⋯⋯ BDE S1 submits weekly AWOL-DFR report to DIV G1 with the AWOL SM's information added.

⋯⋯ PMO will initiate a MP report and blotter entry.

⋯⋯ Unit supply will inventory and secure all SM's personal/government property. Retain copy of inventory in unit files.

CDR / 1SG prepares and mails letter to SM's NOK on 10th day of AWOL informing him/her of the SM's AWOL status.

BN and BDE S1 monitors suspense to ensure DFR action is accomplished in a timely manner.

⋯⋯ As DFR suspense nears, recommend unit begin completing DFR packet to expedite processing on 31st day.

CDR/1SG prepares and mails letter to SM's NOK on 31st day of AWOL informing him/her of the SM's AWOL status.

On 31st day, eMILPO transaction is made changing SM's status from AWOL to DFR.

⋯⋯ Day 31 of AWOL = Day 1 of DFR

REFERENCES:
AR 630-10
MILPER Message 10-241

FLOW CHARTS

DFR

```
                                                    ┌─────────────┐
                                                    │   AWOL      │
                                                    │ Soldier is  │
                                                    │    DFR      │
                                                    └─────────────┘
                                                           │
                                                           ▼
```

Unit appoints a Deserter Control Officer.

↓

CDR / 1SG submits a DD Form 553 through the Provost Marshal and sends completed form to the Installation DCO and U.S. Army Deserter Information Point (USADIP).

↓

Unit immediately notifies Military Police and finance office regarding SM's status. ······· SEE ALARACT 366/2011

↓

BDE S1 verifies SM's necessary documents are uploaded in iPERMS to include: DD Form 93 (Emergency Data), DD Forms 4/1,2,3 (Enlistment / Re-enlistment Contract), DD Form 1966 (Record of Military Processing), and SF 86 (Questionnaire for National Security Positions).

↓

BDE S1 scans completed DFR packet (with only the appropriate enclosures) to the Installation DCO and USADIP NLT 5 days after 31st day of SM's AWOL status. ······· Appropriate enclosures consist of: DA Form 4187 (PDY to AWOL), DA Form 4187 (AWOL to DFR), DD Form 458 (Charge Sheet), 10 day NOK letter, and 31 day NOK letter.

↓

Upon review, USADIP will return DA 4187 (PDY to AWOL), DA Form 4187 (AWOL to DFR within 48 hours), DD Form 458, 10 day NOK letter, and 31 day NOK letter to unit to upload into iPERMS. ······· File Court Martial charges along with all other charges on DD 458

↓

Upon notification, unit picks up deserter returnee packet from Installation DCO and disseminates as appropriate. ······· BDE S1 reconciles and submits weekly AWOL/DFR report; submits to Installation DCO.

REFERENCES:
AR 630-10
MILPER Message 10-241

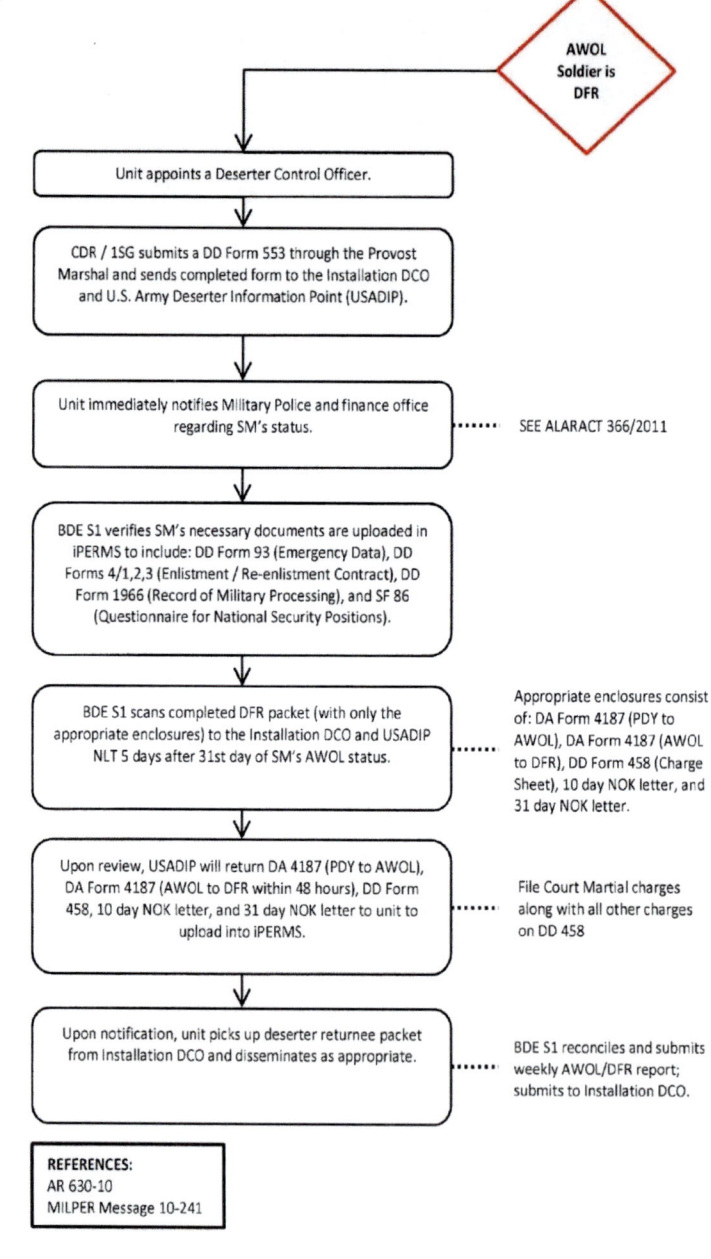

AWOL / DFR INV.

```
◇ AWOL/DFR Clothing Inventory
```

Property must be inventoried as soon as Soldier is discovered absent. AR 700-84 Para 12-13 states, "The abandoned property of an AWOL Soldier will be inventoried without delay." It is recommended clothing is inventoried NLT 72 hours after discovery. Inventory must be completed by E5 (+), O2 (+), or WO. These procedures apply only if the enlisted Soldier resides in troop billets. Another member of the unit must witness inventory.

Inventory officer will:
- Ensure clothing is not exchanged for clothing of any other enlisted Soldier.
- Prepare a DA Form 3078 in triplicate. Record on DA 3078 the items and quantities of personal military clothing issued. Excess personal military clothing above authorized levels will not be recorded on DA Form 3078. These items will be included on the personal effects inventory. See DA Pam 600–8 for instructions on how privately owned military personal property is inventoried. The person conducting the inventory will enter the words "Inventoried by" and sign in the REMARKS block of the DA Form 3078.

The witness, and the unit commander or designated representative, will verify and initial this form. Place the original copy of the inventory in the enlisted Soldier's duffel bag or other suitable container. Retain the other three copies in the unit suspense file pending further action.

Return of the absent enlisted Soldier:
Clothing is returned to the absentee should he or she return to the unit or organization before being dropped from the rolls. The enlisted Soldier will acknowledge receipt of the clothing by signing all copies of DA Form 3078. The enlisted Soldier will be given copy three of the inventory. The unit Commander determines whether the enlisted Soldier has the initial allowances of personal clothing. Shortages are replaced at the Soldier's expense.

REFERENCES:
AR 700-84
DA Pam 600-8

Suicide Ideation / Attempt

```
                                    ┌─────────────────┐
                                    │ SUICIDE         │
                                    │ IDEATION        │
                                    │ / ATTEMPT       │
                                    └─────────────────┘
                                            │
                                            ▼
```

- Immediate Chain of Command informs Company Commander / 1SG

↓

- Cdr / 1SG ensures individual is assessed at WBMC ED or nearest medical facility

↓

- Cdr / 1SG informs higher headquarters and initiates written SIR; conducts verbal Div CCIR notification.

↓

- Cdr / 1SG informs Chaplain and Brigade Behavioral Health Officer to initiate tracking of care and assist in risk management

↓

- Cdr / 1SG address external issues --- access to weapons, unit relationships, financial stressors, others

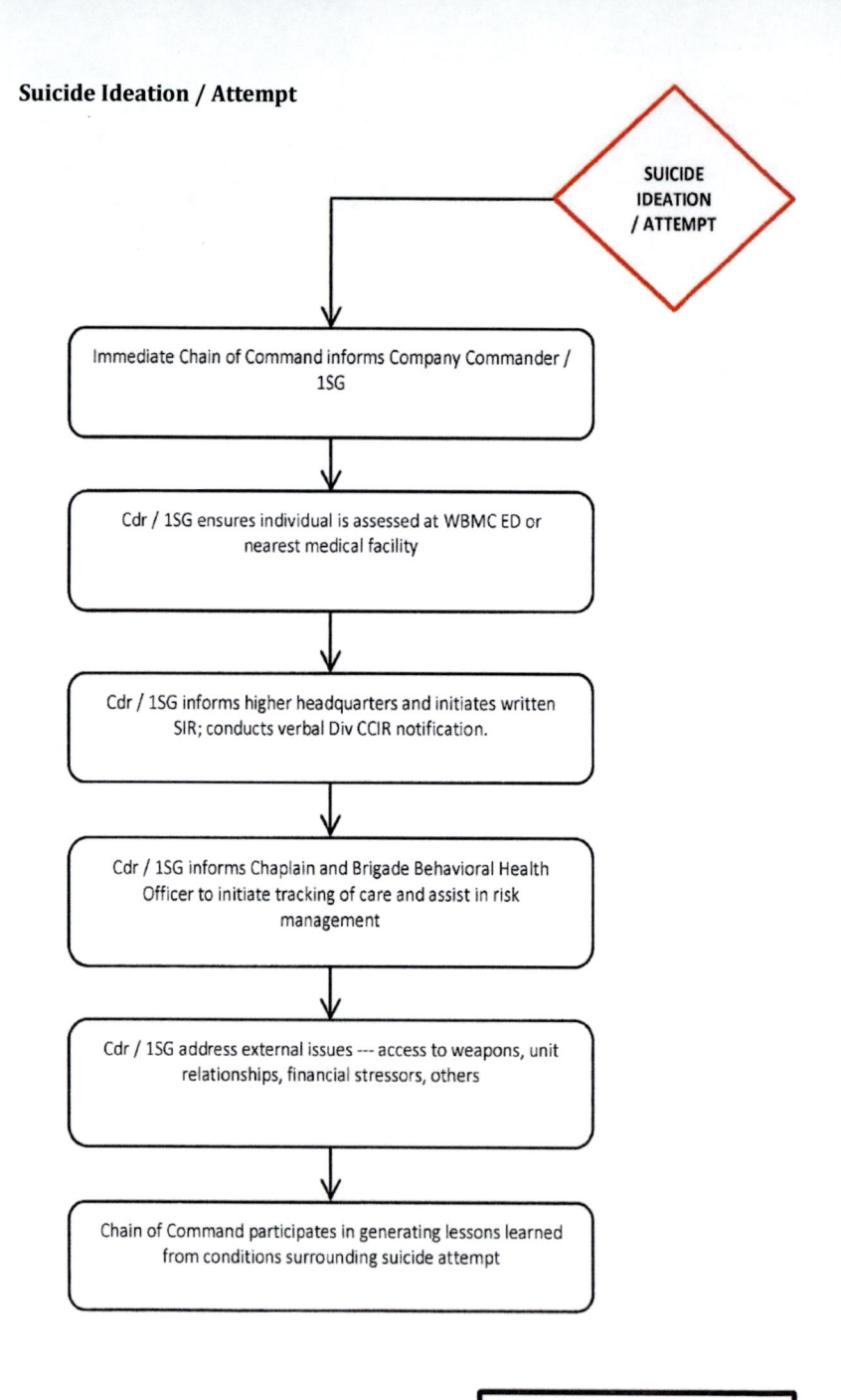

↓

- Chain of Command participates in generating lessons learned from conditions surrounding suicide attempt

REFERENCES:
GTA 12-01-001, Army Suicide Prevention Program

Positive UA

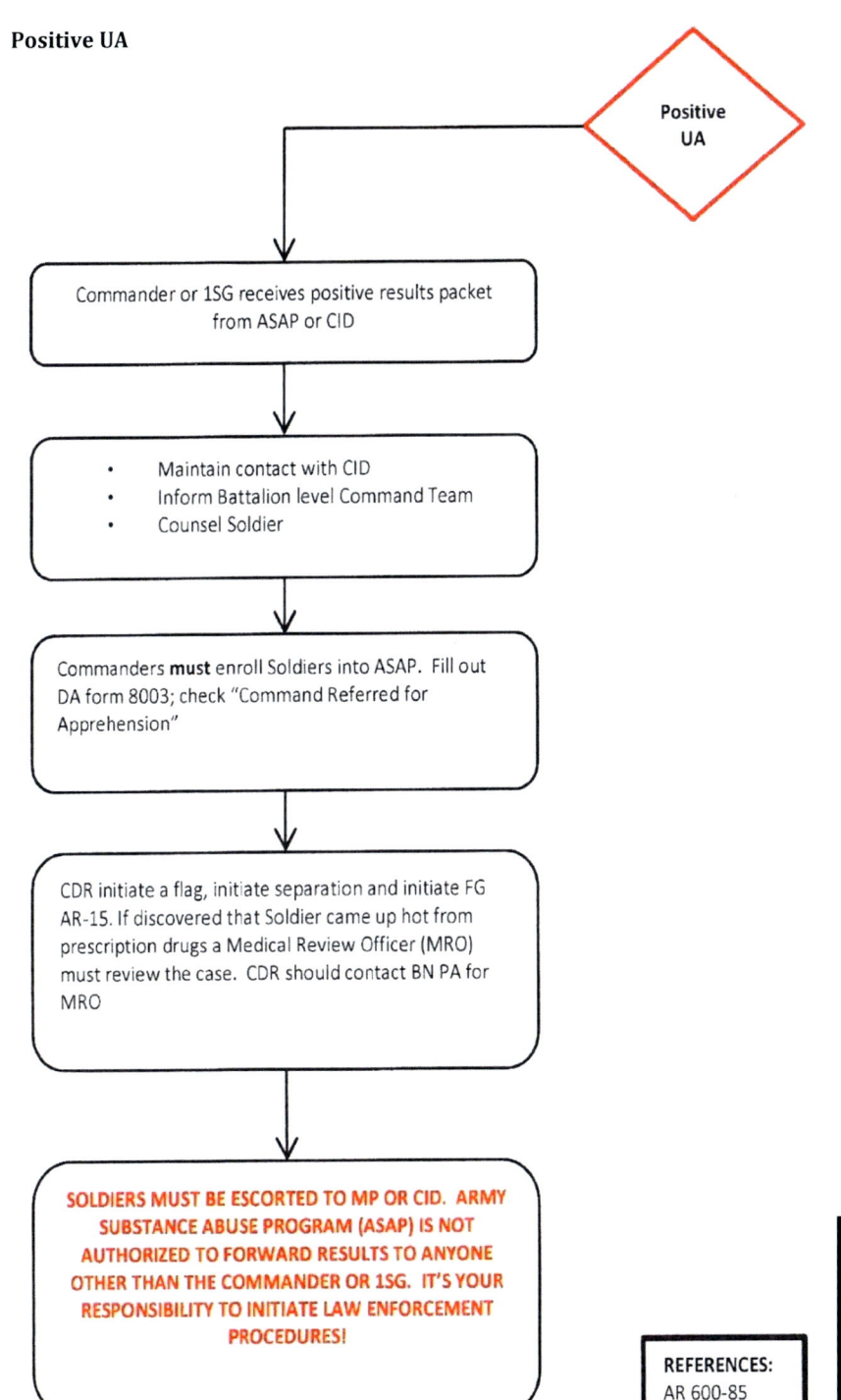

```
                                    ┌─────────────┐
                                    │  Positive   │
                                    │     UA      │
                                    └──────┬──────┘
                                           │
          ┌────────────────────────────────┘
          ▼
┌──────────────────────────────────────────────┐
│ Commander or 1SG receives positive results   │
│ packet from ASAP or CID                      │
└──────────────────┬───────────────────────────┘
                   ▼
┌──────────────────────────────────────────────┐
│   • Maintain contact with CID                │
│   • Inform Battalion level Command Team      │
│   • Counsel Soldier                          │
└──────────────────┬───────────────────────────┘
                   ▼
┌──────────────────────────────────────────────┐
│ Commanders **must** enroll Soldiers into     │
│ ASAP. Fill out DA form 8003; check "Command  │
│ Referred for Apprehension"                   │
└──────────────────┬───────────────────────────┘
                   ▼
┌──────────────────────────────────────────────┐
│ CDR initiate a flag, initiate separation and │
│ initiate FG AR-15. If discovered that        │
│ Soldier came up hot from prescription drugs  │
│ a Medical Review Officer (MRO) must review   │
│ the case. CDR should contact BN PA for MRO   │
└──────────────────┬───────────────────────────┘
                   ▼
┌──────────────────────────────────────────────┐
│ **SOLDIERS MUST BE ESCORTED TO MP OR CID.    │
│ ARMY SUBSTANCE ABUSE PROGRAM (ASAP) IS NOT   │
│ AUTHORIZED TO FORWARD RESULTS TO ANYONE      │
│ OTHER THAN THE COMMANDER OR 1SG. IT'S YOUR   │
│ RESPONSIBILITY TO INITIATE LAW ENFORCEMENT   │
│ PROCEDURES!**                                │
└──────────────────────────────────────────────┘
```

REFERENCES: AR 600-85

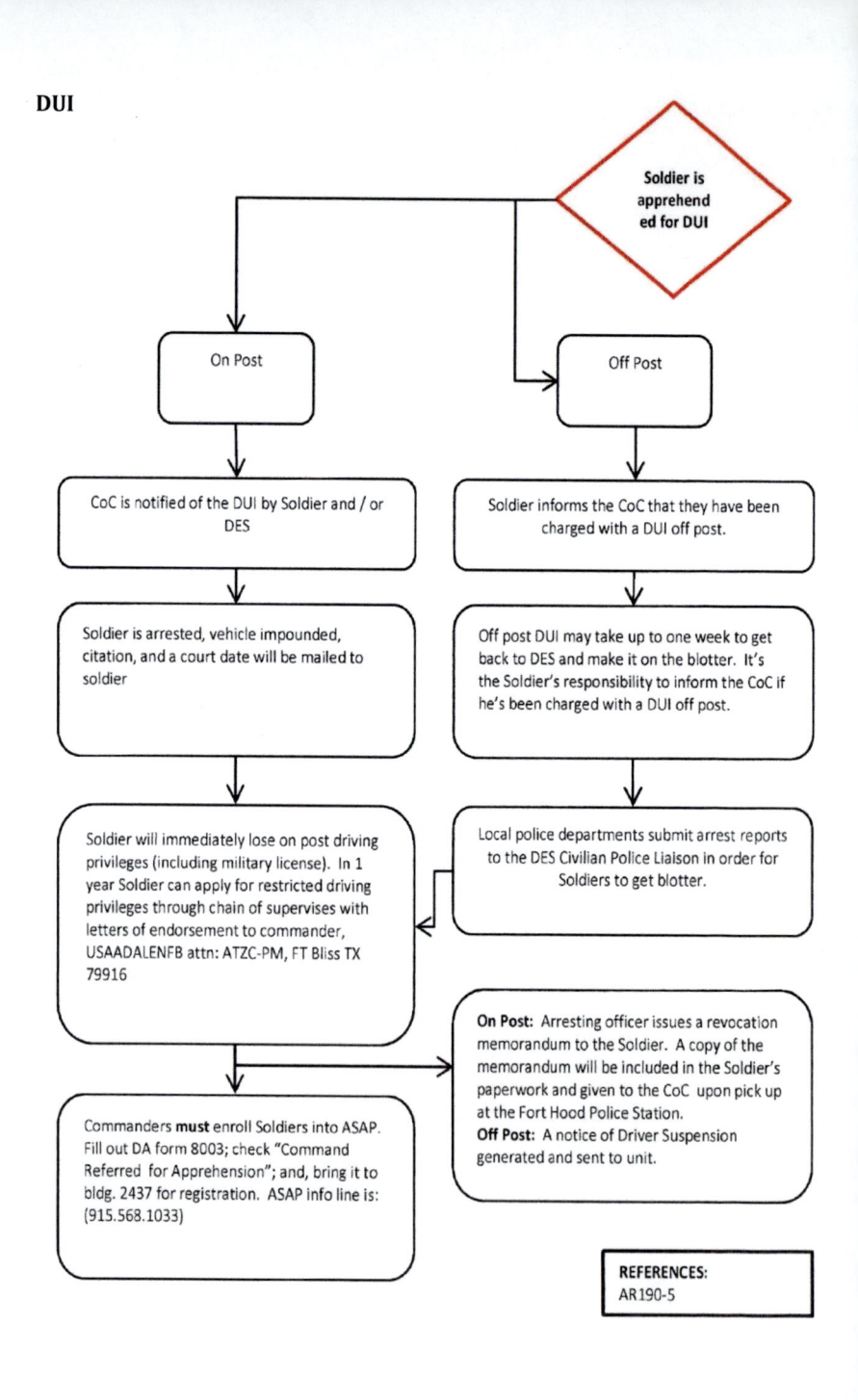

DUI

```
                                    ┌─────────────────┐
                                    │  Soldier is     │
                                    │  apprehended    │
                                    │  for DUI        │
                                    └─────────────────┘
```

Soldier is apprehended for DUI → branches to **On Post** and **Off Post**

On Post

- CoC is notified of the DUI by Soldier and / or DES
- Soldier is arrested, vehicle impounded, citation, and a court date will be mailed to soldier
- Soldier will immediately lose on post driving privileges (including military license). In 1 year Soldier can apply for restricted driving privileges through chain of supervises with letters of endorsement to commander, USAADALENFB attn: ATZC-PM, FT Bliss TX 79916
- Commanders **must** enroll Soldiers into ASAP. Fill out DA form 8003; check "Command Referred for Apprehension"; and, bring it to bldg. 2437 for registration. ASAP info line is: (915.568.1033)

Off Post

- Soldier informs the CoC that they have been charged with a DUI off post.
- Off post DUI may take up to one week to get back to DES and make it on the blotter. It's the Soldier's responsibility to inform the CoC if he's been charged with a DUI off post.
- Local police departments submit arrest reports to the DES Civilian Police Liaison in order for Soldiers to get blotter.
- **On Post:** Arresting officer issues a revocation memorandum to the Soldier. A copy of the memorandum will be included in the Soldier's paperwork and given to the CoC upon pick up at the Fort Hood Police Station.
- **Off Post:** A notice of Driver Suspension generated and sent to unit.

REFERENCES:
AR 190-5

Domestic Abuse

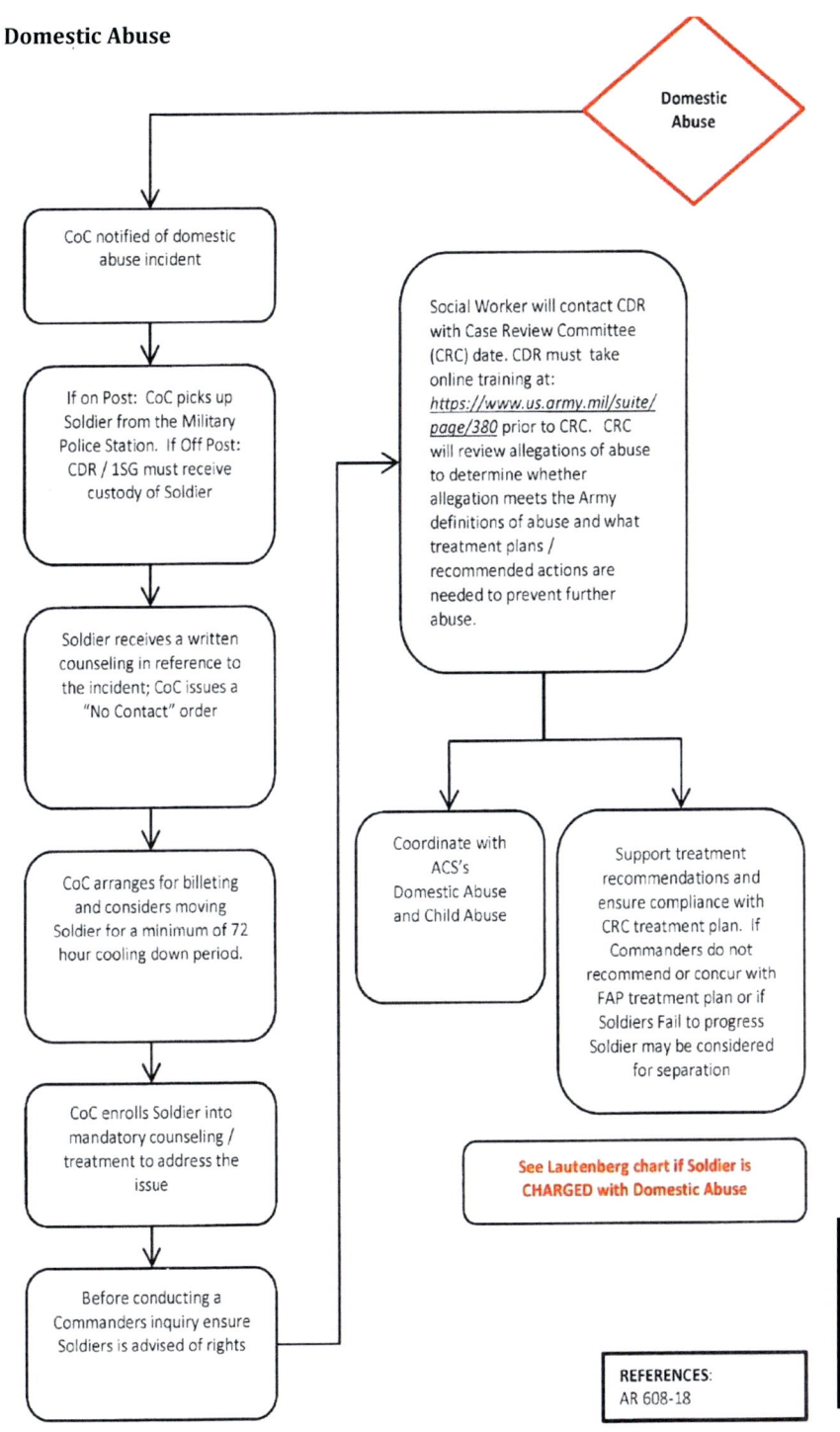

Domestic Abuse (decision)

- CoC notified of domestic abuse incident
- If on Post: CoC picks up Soldier from the Military Police Station. If Off Post: CDR / 1SG must receive custody of Soldier
- Soldier receives a written counseling in reference to the incident; CoC issues a "No Contact" order
- CoC arranges for billeting and considers moving Soldier for a minimum of 72 hour cooling down period.
- CoC enrolls Soldier into mandatory counseling / treatment to address the issue
- Before conducting a Commanders inquiry ensure Soldiers is advised of rights

Social Worker will contact CDR with Case Review Committee (CRC) date. CDR must take online training at: https://www.us.army.mil/suite/page/380 prior to CRC. CRC will review allegations of abuse to determine whether allegation meets the Army definitions of abuse and what treatment plans / recommended actions are needed to prevent further abuse.

- Coordinate with ACS's Domestic Abuse and Child Abuse
- Support treatment recommendations and ensure compliance with CRC treatment plan. If Commanders do not recommend or concur with FAP treatment plan or if Soldiers Fail to progress Soldier may be considered for separation

See Lautenberg chart if Soldier is CHARGED with Domestic Abuse

REFERENCES:
AR 608-18

Lautenberg Amendment

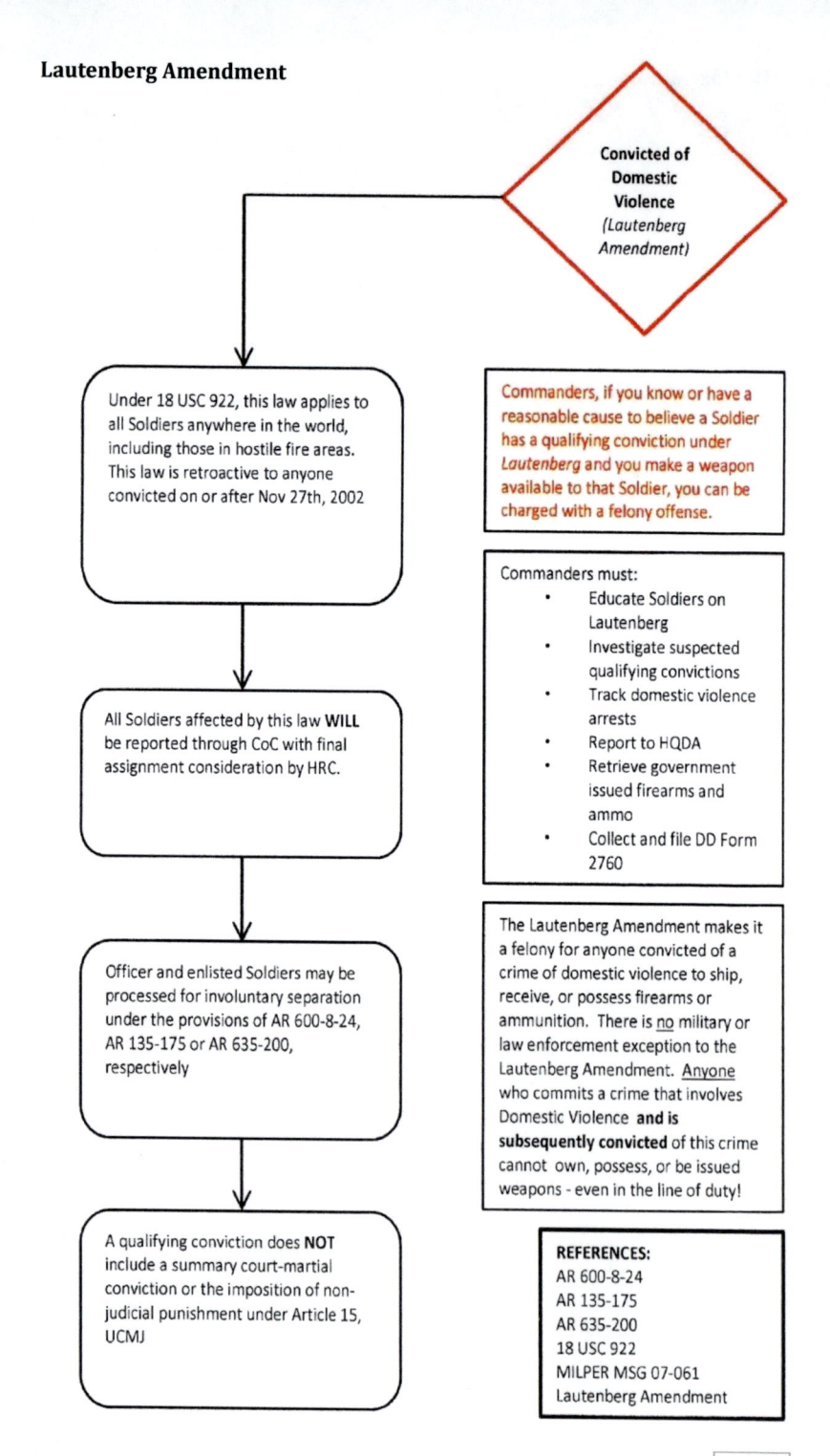

```
                    ◇ Convicted of
                      Domestic
                      Violence
                      (Lautenberg
                      Amendment)
```

Under 18 USC 922, this law applies to all Soldiers anywhere in the world, including those in hostile fire areas. This law is retroactive to anyone convicted on or after Nov 27th, 2002

All Soldiers affected by this law **WILL** be reported through CoC with final assignment consideration by HRC.

Officer and enlisted Soldiers may be processed for involuntary separation under the provisions of AR 600-8-24, AR 135-175 or AR 635-200, respectively

A qualifying conviction does **NOT** include a summary court-martial conviction or the imposition of non-judicial punishment under Article 15, UCMJ

Commanders, if you know or have a reasonable cause to believe a Soldier has a qualifying conviction under *Lautenberg* and you make a weapon available to that Soldier, you can be charged with a felony offense.

Commanders must:
- Educate Soldiers on Lautenberg
- Investigate suspected qualifying convictions
- Track domestic violence arrests
- Report to HQDA
- Retrieve government issued firearms and ammo
- Collect and file DD Form 2760

The Lautenberg Amendment makes it a felony for anyone convicted of a crime of domestic violence to ship, receive, or possess firearms or ammunition. There is <u>no</u> military or law enforcement exception to the Lautenberg Amendment. <u>Anyone</u> who commits a crime that involves Domestic Violence **and is subsequently convicted** of this crime cannot own, possess, or be issued weapons - even in the line of duty!

REFERENCES:
AR 600-8-24
AR 135-175
AR 635-200
18 USC 922
MILPER MSG 07-061
Lautenberg Amendment

Sexual Harassment

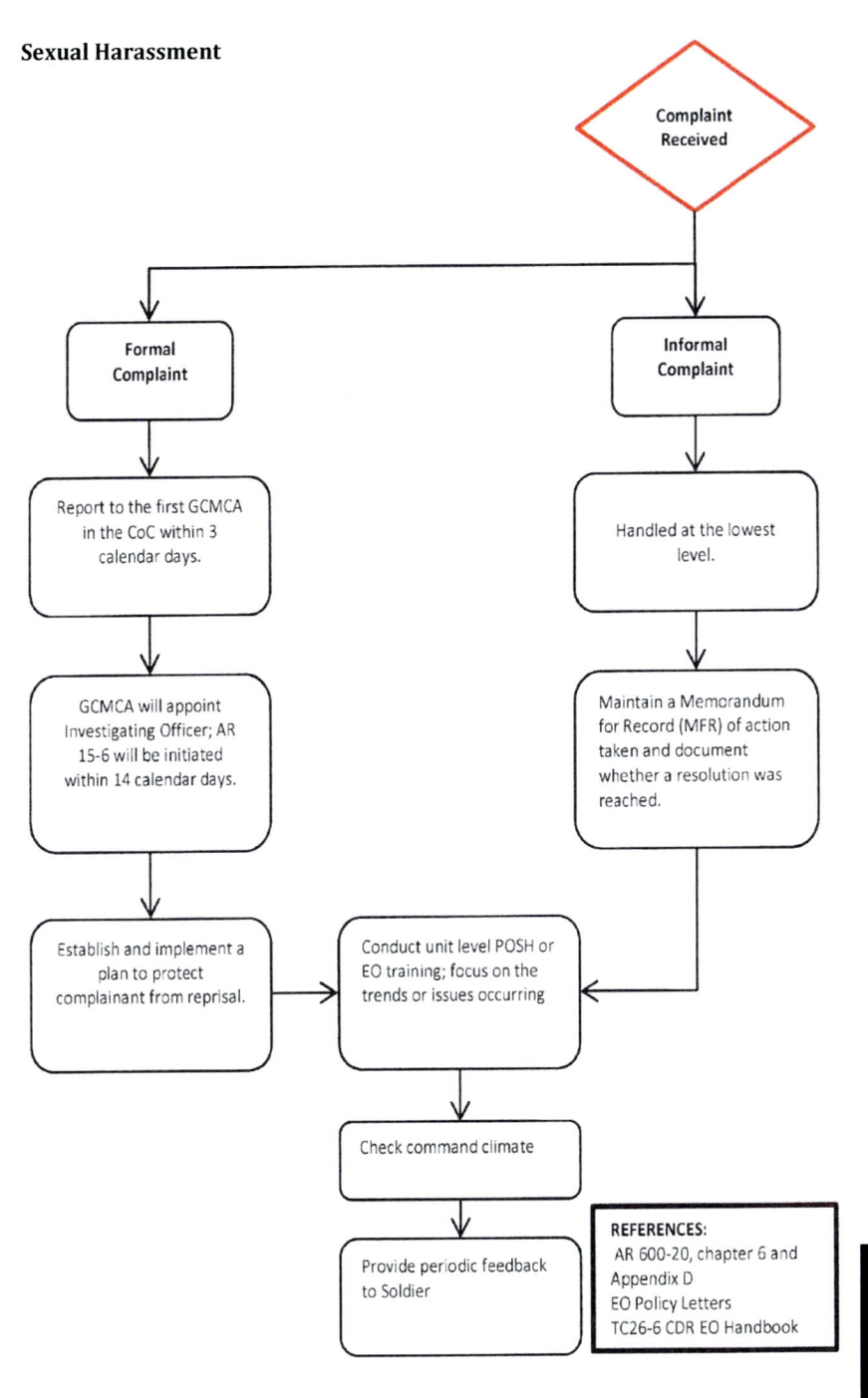

```
                            ┌─────────────┐
                            │  Complaint  │
                            │  Received   │
                            └──────┬──────┘
                    ┌──────────────┴──────────────┐
                    ▼                             ▼
           ┌─────────────┐                 ┌─────────────┐
           │   Formal    │                 │  Informal   │
           │  Complaint  │                 │  Complaint  │
           └──────┬──────┘                 └──────┬──────┘
                  ▼                               ▼
```

Formal Complaint path:
- Report to the first GCMCA in the CoC within 3 calendar days.
- GCMCA will appoint Investigating Officer; AR 15-6 will be initiated within 14 calendar days.
- Establish and implement a plan to protect complainant from reprisal.

Informal Complaint path:
- Handled at the lowest level.
- Maintain a Memorandum for Record (MFR) of action taken and document whether a resolution was reached.

Both paths converge to:
- Conduct unit level POSH or EO training; focus on the trends or issues occurring
- Check command climate
- Provide periodic feedback to Soldier

REFERENCES:
AR 600-20, chapter 6 and Appendix D
EO Policy Letters
TC26-6 CDR EO Handbook

Sexual Assault

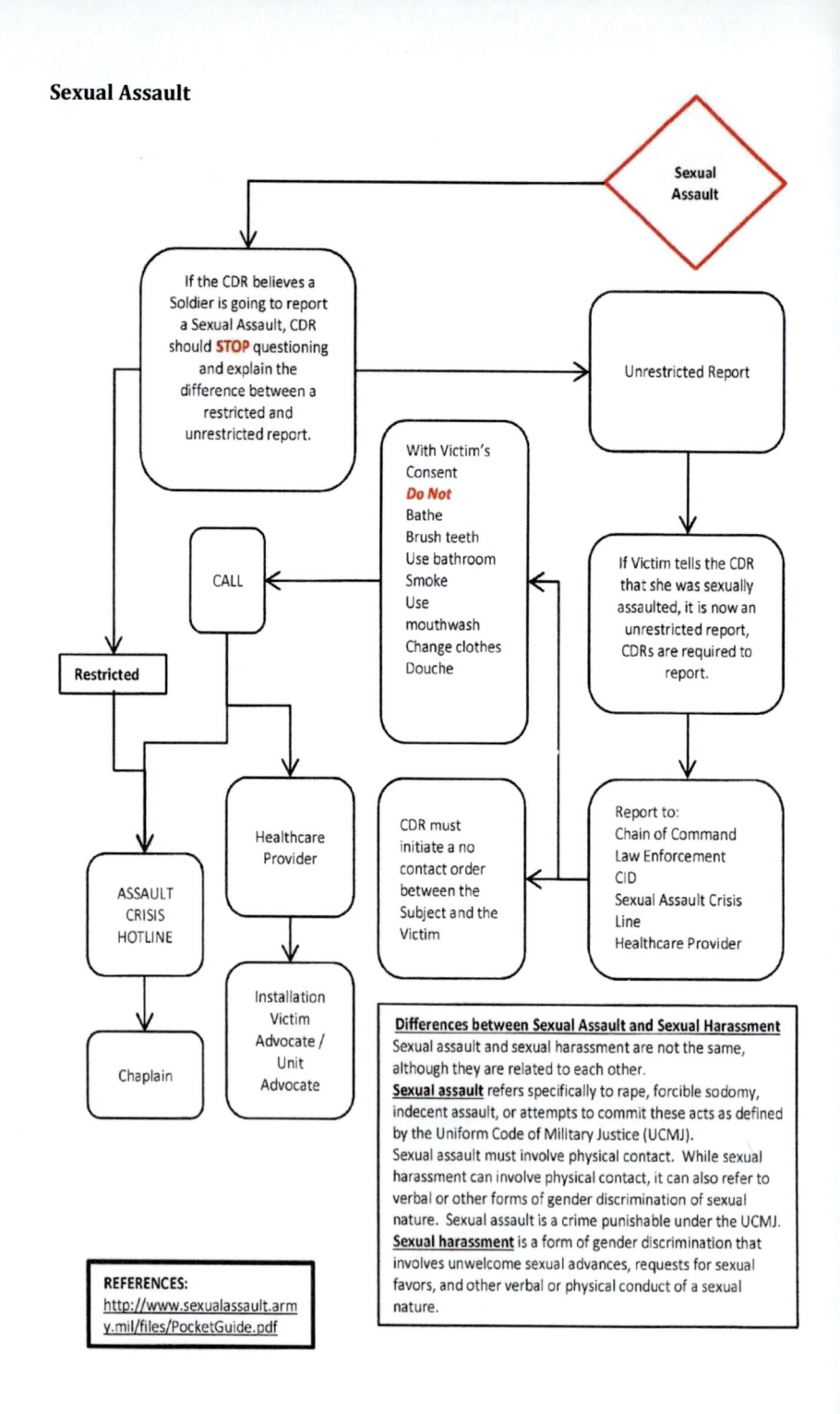

Sexual Assault (decision node)

If the CDR believes a Soldier is going to report a Sexual Assault, CDR should **STOP** questioning and explain the difference between a restricted and unrestricted report.

→ **Unrestricted Report**

With Victim's Consent
Do Not
- Bathe
- Brush teeth
- Use bathroom
- Smoke
- Use mouthwash
- Change clothes
- Douche

CALL

Restricted

If Victim tells the CDR that she was sexually assaulted, it is now an unrestricted report, CDRs are required to report.

- ASSAULT CRISIS HOTLINE
- Healthcare Provider
- CDR must initiate a no contact order between the Subject and the Victim

Report to:
- Chain of Command
- Law Enforcement
- CID
- Sexual Assault Crisis Line
- Healthcare Provider

- Chaplain
- Installation Victim Advocate / Unit Advocate

Differences between Sexual Assault and Sexual Harassment

Sexual assault and sexual harassment are not the same, although they are related to each other.

Sexual assault refers specifically to rape, forcible sodomy, indecent assault, or attempts to commit these acts as defined by the Uniform Code of Military Justice (UCMJ). Sexual assault must involve physical contact. While sexual harassment can involve physical contact, it can also refer to verbal or other forms of gender discrimination of sexual nature. Sexual assault is a crime punishable under the UCMJ.

Sexual harassment is a form of gender discrimination that involves unwelcome sexual advances, requests for sexual favors, and other verbal or physical conduct of a sexual nature.

REFERENCES:
http://www.sexualassault.army.mil/files/PocketGuide.pdf

WTB Nomination

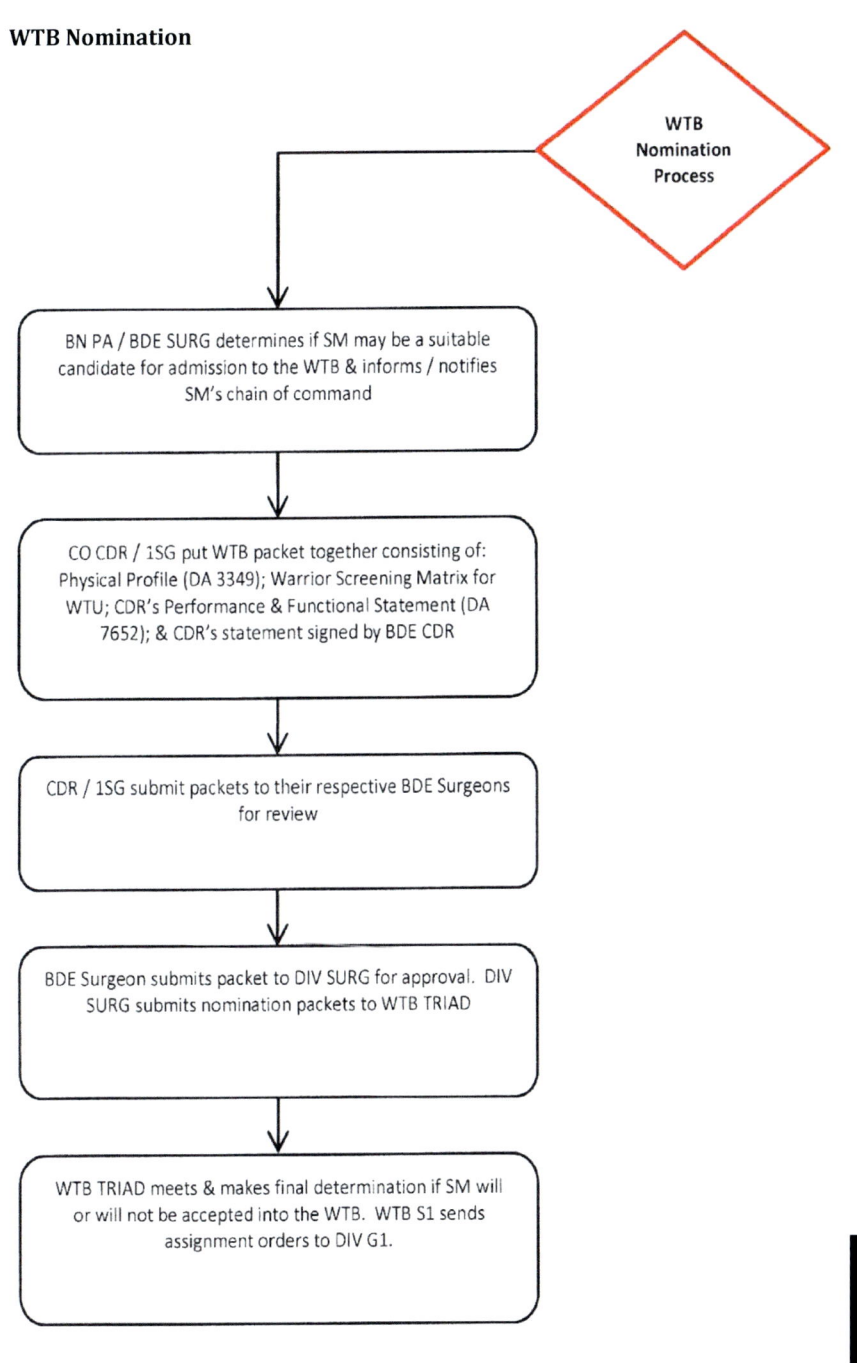

```
                                    ┌─────────────┐
                                    │    WTB      │
                                    │ Nomination  │
                                    │   Process   │
                                    └─────────────┘
                                           │
           ┌───────────────────────────────┘
           ▼
┌──────────────────────────────────────────────┐
│ BN PA / BDE SURG determines if SM may be a   │
│ suitable candidate for admission to the WTB  │
│ & informs / notifies SM's chain of command   │
└──────────────────────────────────────────────┘
           │
           ▼
┌──────────────────────────────────────────────┐
│ CO CDR / 1SG put WTB packet together         │
│ consisting of: Physical Profile (DA 3349);   │
│ Warrior Screening Matrix for WTU; CDR's      │
│ Performance & Functional Statement (DA       │
│ 7652); & CDR's statement signed by BDE CDR   │
└──────────────────────────────────────────────┘
           │
           ▼
┌──────────────────────────────────────────────┐
│ CDR / 1SG submit packets to their respective │
│ BDE Surgeons for review                      │
└──────────────────────────────────────────────┘
           │
           ▼
┌──────────────────────────────────────────────┐
│ BDE Surgeon submits packet to DIV SURG for   │
│ approval. DIV SURG submits nomination        │
│ packets to WTB TRIAD                         │
└──────────────────────────────────────────────┘
           │
           ▼
┌──────────────────────────────────────────────┐
│ WTB TRIAD meets & makes final determination  │
│ if SM will or will not be accepted into the  │
│ WTB. WTB S1 sends assignment orders to       │
│ DIV G1.                                      │
└──────────────────────────────────────────────┘
```

Hospitalization

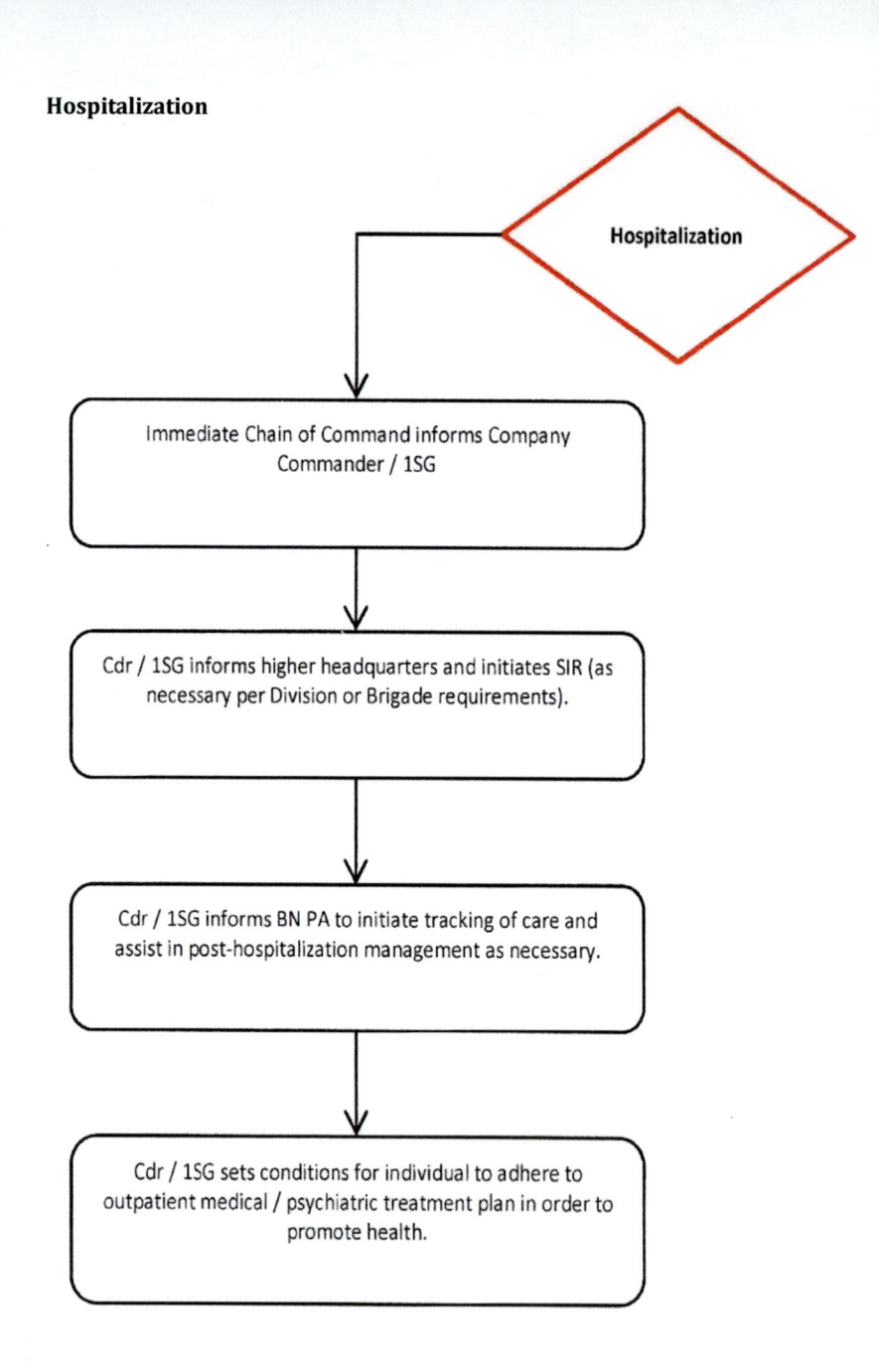

```
                                    ┌─────────────────┐
                                    │ Hospitalization │
                                    └────────┬────────┘
                                             │
                    ┌────────────────────────▼────────────────────────┐
                    │ Immediate Chain of Command informs Company      │
                    │ Commander / 1SG                                 │
                    └────────────────────────┬────────────────────────┘
                                             ▼
                    ┌─────────────────────────────────────────────────┐
                    │ Cdr / 1SG informs higher headquarters and       │
                    │ initiates SIR (as necessary per Division or     │
                    │ Brigade requirements).                          │
                    └────────────────────────┬────────────────────────┘
                                             ▼
                    ┌─────────────────────────────────────────────────┐
                    │ Cdr / 1SG informs BN PA to initiate tracking of │
                    │ care and assist in post-hospitalization         │
                    │ management as necessary.                        │
                    └────────────────────────┬────────────────────────┘
                                             ▼
                    ┌─────────────────────────────────────────────────┐
                    │ Cdr / 1SG sets conditions for individual to     │
                    │ adhere to outpatient medical / psychiatric      │
                    │ treatment plan in order to promote health.      │
                    └─────────────────────────────────────────────────┘
```

Family Care Plan

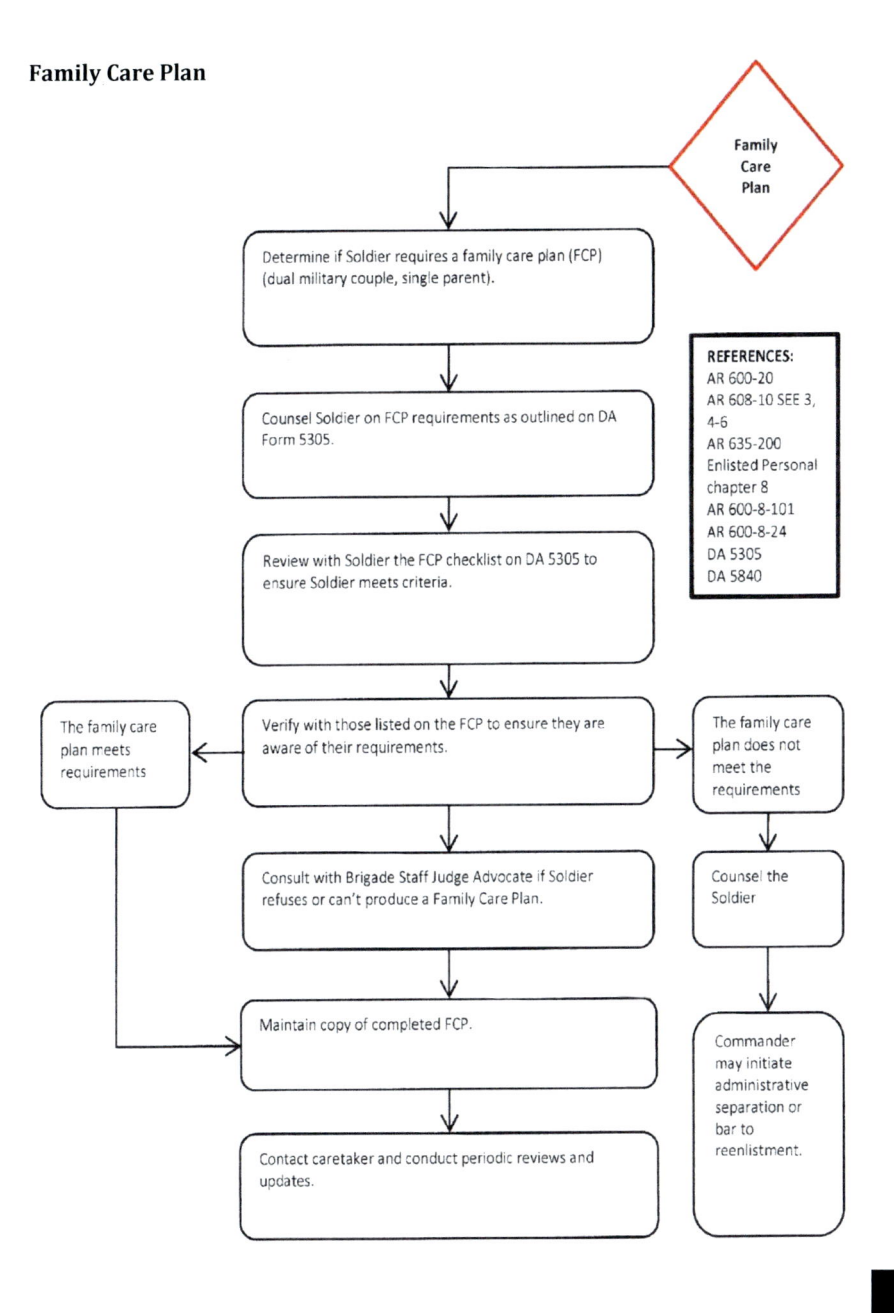

```
                                            ┌─────────┐
                                            │ Family  │
                                            │  Care   │
                                            │  Plan   │
                                            └────┬────┘
                                                 │
                                                 ▼
        ┌──────────────────────────────────────────────┐
        │ Determine if Soldier requires a family care  │
        │ plan (FCP) (dual military couple, single     │
        │ parent).                                     │
        └──────────────────────────────────────────────┘
                            │
                            ▼
        ┌──────────────────────────────────────────────┐
        │ Counsel Soldier on FCP requirements as       │
        │ outlined on DA Form 5305.                    │
        └──────────────────────────────────────────────┘
                            │
                            ▼
        ┌──────────────────────────────────────────────┐
        │ Review with Soldier the FCP checklist on DA  │
        │ 5305 to ensure Soldier meets criteria.       │
        └──────────────────────────────────────────────┘
```

REFERENCES:
AR 600-20
AR 608-10 SEE 3, 4-6
AR 635-200 Enlisted Personal chapter 8
AR 600-8-101
AR 600-8-24
DA 5305
DA 5840

- The family care plan meets requirements ← Verify with those listed on the FCP to ensure they are aware of their requirements. → The family care plan does not meet the requirements

- Consult with Brigade Staff Judge Advocate if Soldier refuses or can't produce a Family Care Plan.

- Counsel the Soldier

- Maintain copy of completed FCP.

- Commander may initiate administrative separation or bar to reenlistment.

- Contact caretaker and conduct periodic reviews and updates.

FLOW CHARTS

Suspense of Favorable Actions

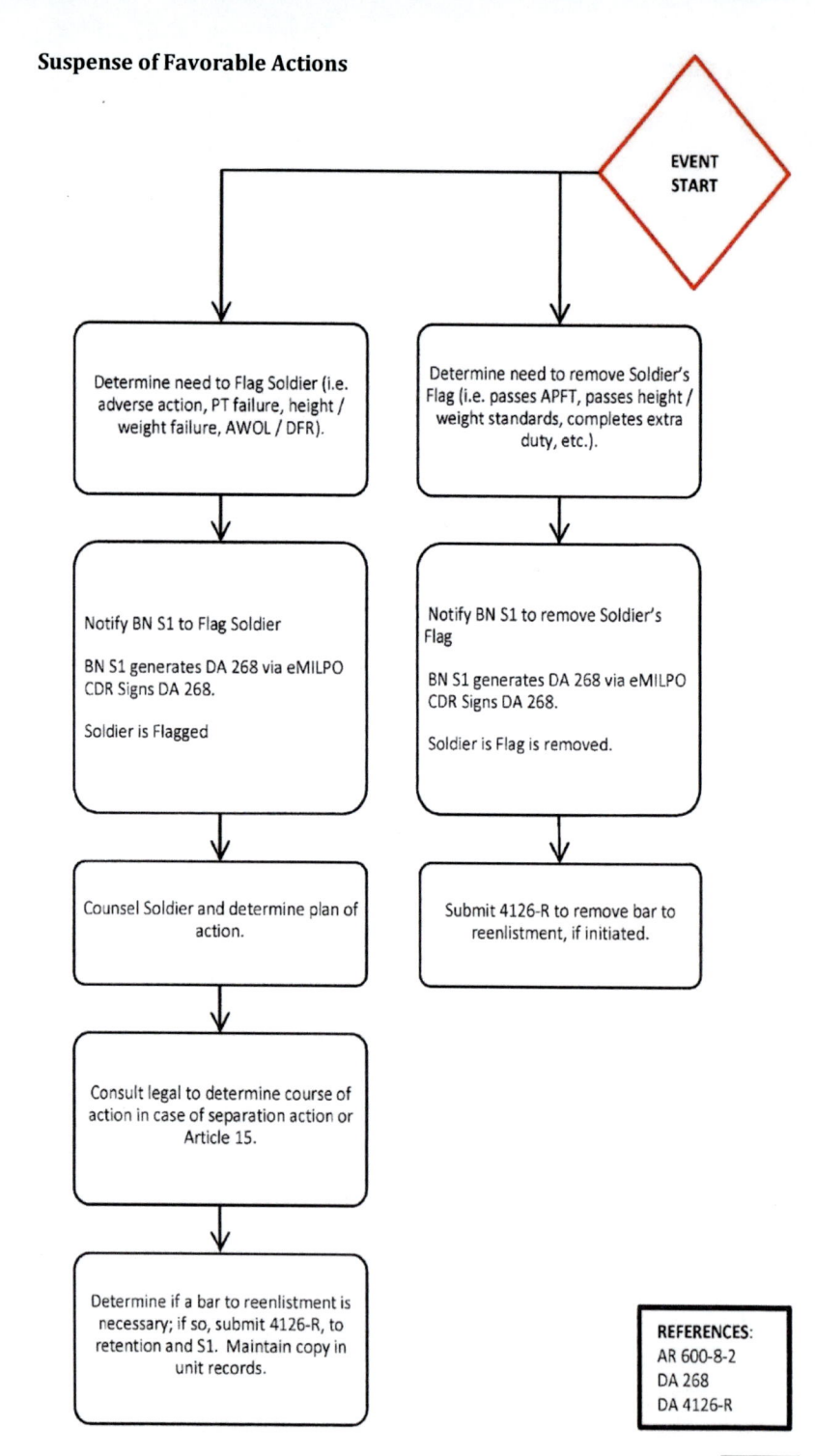

EVENT START

- Determine need to Flag Soldier (i.e. adverse action, PT failure, height / weight failure, AWOL / DFR).

- Notify BN S1 to Flag Soldier

  BN S1 generates DA 268 via eMILPO CDR Signs DA 268.

  Soldier is Flagged

- Counsel Soldier and determine plan of action.

- Consult legal to determine course of action in case of separation action or Article 15.

- Determine if a bar to reenlistment is necessary; if so, submit 4126-R, to retention and S1. Maintain copy in unit records.

- Determine need to remove Soldier's Flag (i.e. passes APFT, passes height / weight standards, completes extra duty, etc.).

- Notify BN S1 to remove Soldier's Flag

  BN S1 generates DA 268 via eMILPO CDR Signs DA 268.

  Soldier is Flag is removed.

- Submit 4126-R to remove bar to reenlistment, if initiated.

REFERENCES:
AR 600-8-2
DA 268
DA 4126-R

Bar to Reenlistment

```
                                    ┌─────────┐
                                    │ Initiate│
                                    │   Bar   │
                                    └─────────┘
                                         │
                                         ▼
```

Determine need for the Bar to Reenlistment. Bar to Reenlistment can be initiated for: APFT Failure, Poor Performance, Height / Weight Failure, or even Commander's discretion. If a Commander determines a Soldier's performance does not warrant reenlistment in the US Army, they need to submit 4126-R to Retention and the BN S1. Maintain a copy in unit records..

REFERENCES:
AR 601-280 (CH. 8)
DA 4126-R

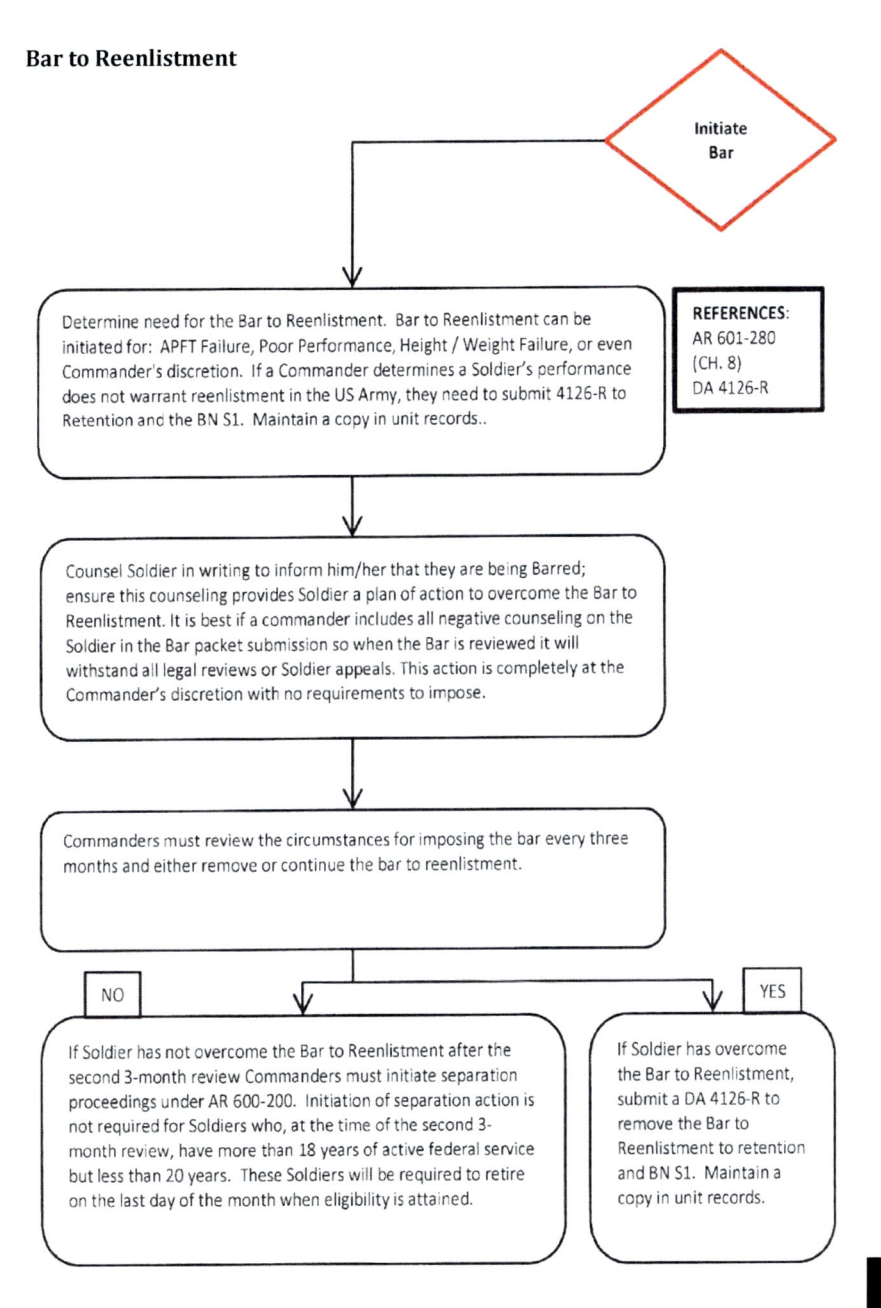

Counsel Soldier in writing to inform him/her that they are being Barred; ensure this counseling provides Soldier a plan of action to overcome the Bar to Reenlistment. It is best if a commander includes all negative counseling on the Soldier in the Bar packet submission so when the Bar is reviewed it will withstand all legal reviews or Soldier appeals. This action is completely at the Commander's discretion with no requirements to impose.

Commanders must review the circumstances for imposing the bar every three months and either remove or continue the bar to reenlistment.

NO

If Soldier has not overcome the Bar to Reenlistment after the second 3-month review Commanders must initiate separation proceedings under AR 600-200. Initiation of separation action is not required for Soldiers who, at the time of the second 3-month review, have more than 18 years of active federal service but less than 20 years. These Soldiers will be required to retire on the last day of the month when eligibility is attained.

YES

If Soldier has overcome the Bar to Reenlistment, submit a DA 4126-R to remove the Bar to Reenlistment to retention and BN S1. Maintain a copy in unit records.

FLOW CHARTS

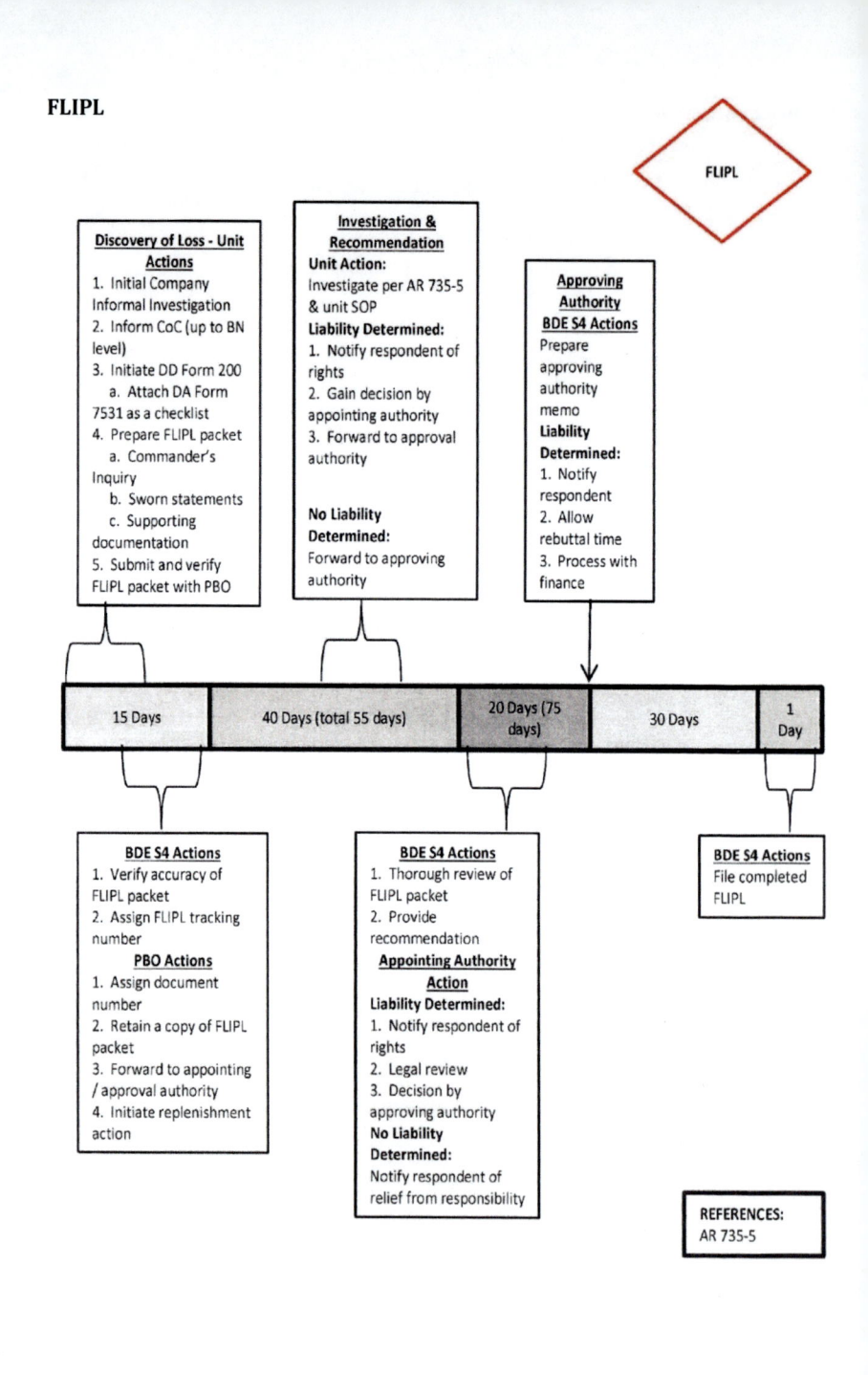

FLIPL

FLIPL

Discovery of Loss - Unit Actions
1. Initial Company Informal Investigation
2. Inform CoC (up to BN level)
3. Initiate DD Form 200
   a. Attach DA Form 7531 as a checklist
4. Prepare FLIPL packet
   a. Commander's Inquiry
   b. Sworn statements
   c. Supporting documentation
5. Submit and verify FLIPL packet with PBO

Investigation & Recommendation
Unit Action: Investigate per AR 735-5 & unit SOP

Liability Determined:
1. Notify respondent of rights
2. Gain decision by appointing authority
3. Forward to approval authority

No Liability Determined: Forward to approving authority

Approving Authority
BDE S4 Actions Prepare approving authority memo

Liability Determined:
1. Notify respondent
2. Allow rebuttal time
3. Process with finance

Timeline: 15 Days | 40 Days (total 55 days) | 20 Days (75 days) | 30 Days | 1 Day

---

BDE S4 Actions
1. Verify accuracy of FLIPL packet
2. Assign FLIPL tracking number

PBO Actions
1. Assign document number
2. Retain a copy of FLIPL packet
3. Forward to appointing / approval authority
4. Initiate replenishment action

BDE S4 Actions
1. Thorough review of FLIPL packet
2. Provide recommendation

Appointing Authority Action
Liability Determined:
1. Notify respondent of rights
2. Legal review
3. Decision by approving authority

No Liability Determined: Notify respondent of relief from responsibility

BDE S4 Actions
File completed FLIPL

REFERENCES: AR 735-5

Soldier Death

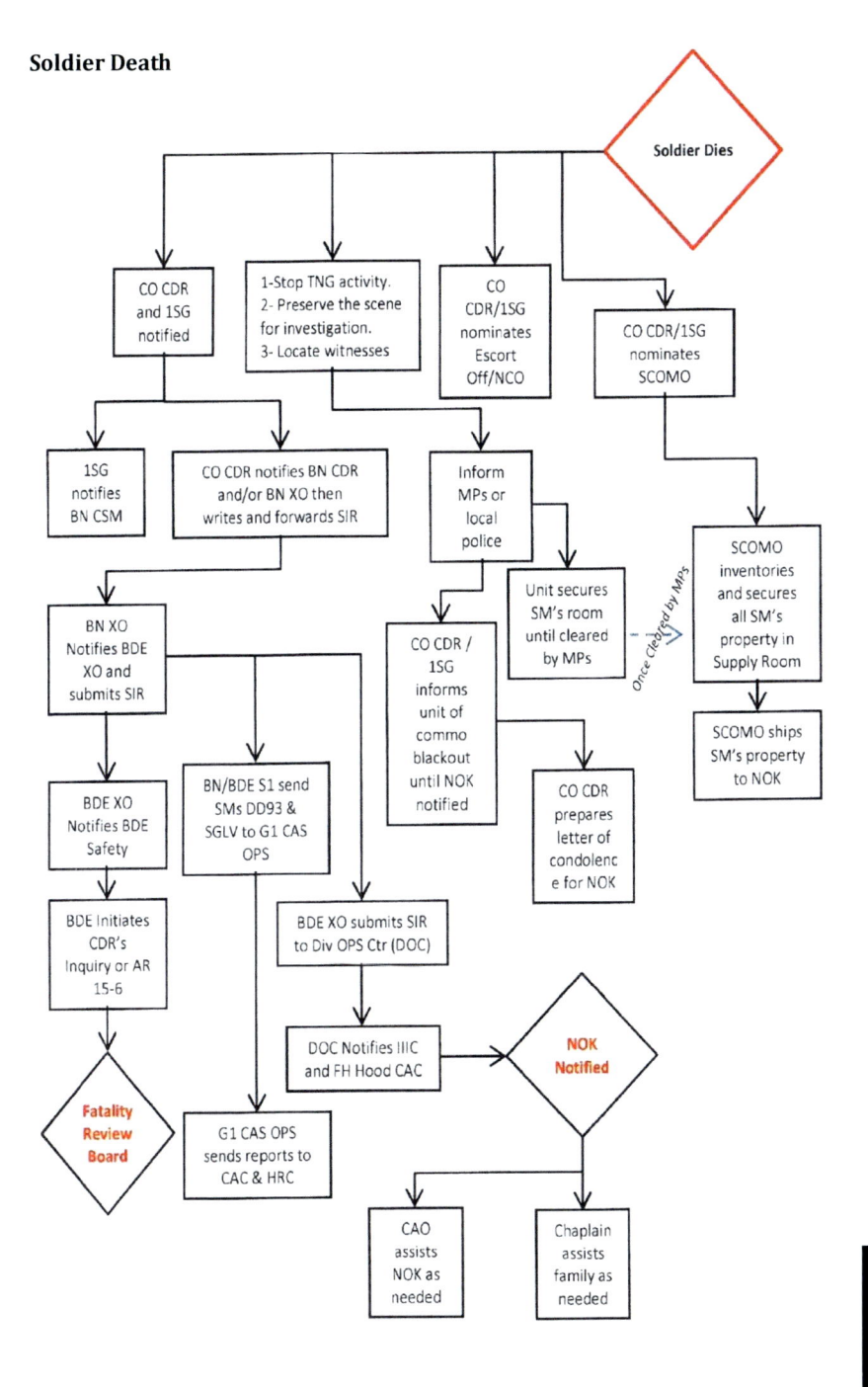

Soldier Dies

- CO CDR and 1SG notified
- 1- Stop TNG activity. 2- Preserve the scene for investigation. 3- Locate witnesses
- CO CDR/1SG nominates Escort Off/NCO
- CO CDR/1SG nominates SCOMO

- 1SG notifies BN CSM
- CO CDR notifies BN CDR and/or BN XO then writes and forwards SIR
- Inform MPs or local police
- Unit secures SM's room until cleared by MPs (Once cleared by MPs)
- SCOMO inventories and secures all SM's property in Supply Room
- SCOMO ships SM's property to NOK

- BN XO Notifies BDE XO and submits SIR
- CO CDR / 1SG informs unit of commo blackout until NOK notified
- CO CDR prepares letter of condolence for NOK

- BDE XO Notifies BDE Safety
- BN/BDE S1 send SMs DD93 & SGLV to G1 CAS OPS
- BDE XO submits SIR to Div OPS Ctr (DOC)

- BDE Initiates CDR's Inquiry or AR 15-6
- DOC Notifies IIIC and FH Hood CAC
- **NOK Notified**

- **Fatality Review Board**
- G1 CAS OPS sends reports to CAC & HRC
- CAO assists NOK as needed
- Chaplain assists family as needed

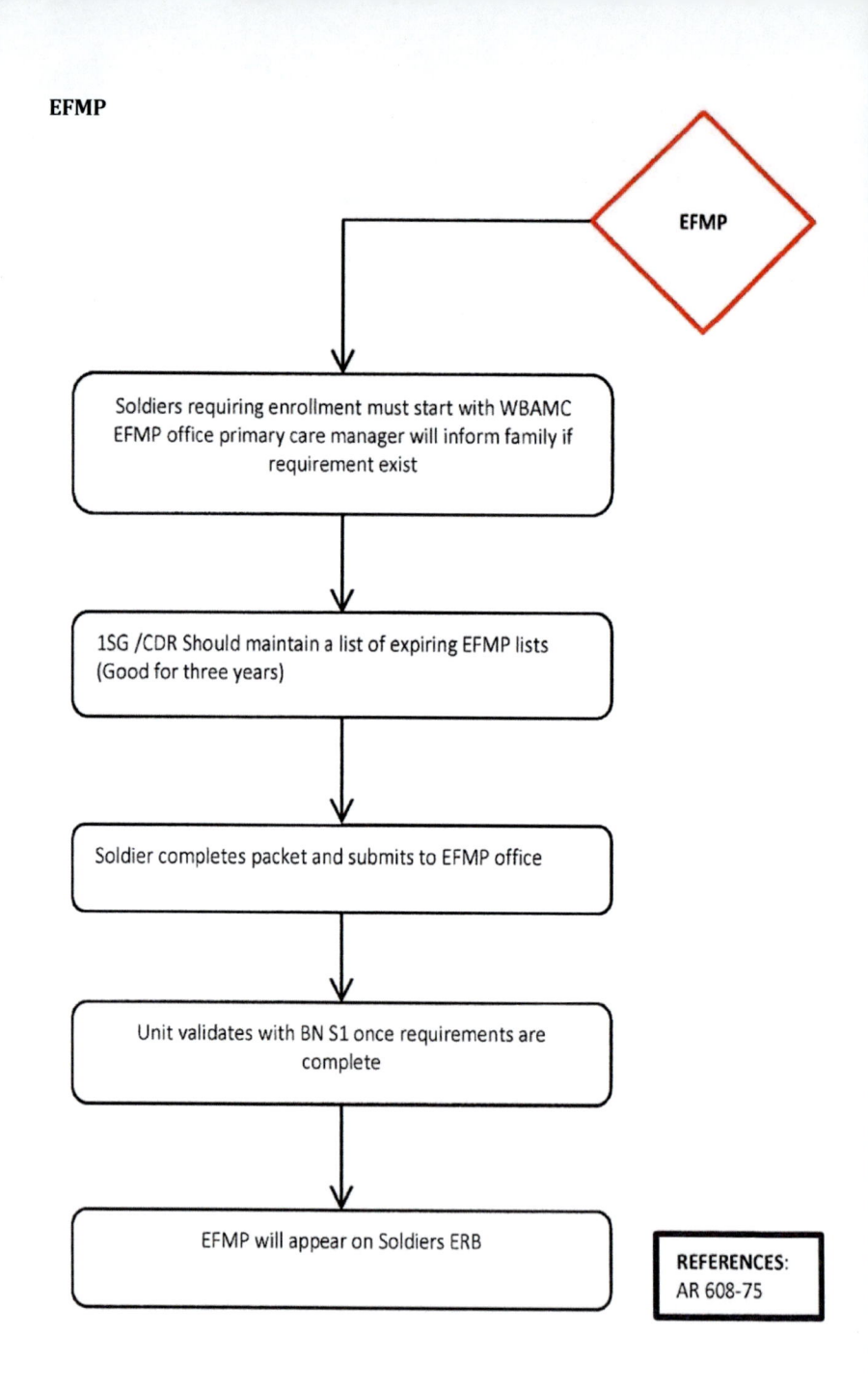

EFMP

```
                              ┌─────────┐
                              │  EFMP   │
                              └────┬────┘
                                   │
                                   ▼
┌─────────────────────────────────────────────────────┐
│ Soldiers requiring enrollment must start with WBAMC │
│ EFMP office primary care manager will inform family │
│                 if requirement exist                │
└─────────────────────┬───────────────────────────────┘
                      │
                      ▼
┌─────────────────────────────────────────────────────┐
│ 1SG /CDR Should maintain a list of expiring EFMP    │
│ lists (Good for three years)                        │
└─────────────────────┬───────────────────────────────┘
                      │
                      ▼
┌─────────────────────────────────────────────────────┐
│ Soldier completes packet and submits to EFMP office │
└─────────────────────┬───────────────────────────────┘
                      │
                      ▼
┌─────────────────────────────────────────────────────┐
│ Unit validates with BN S1 once requirements are     │
│ complete                                            │
└─────────────────────┬───────────────────────────────┘
                      │
                      ▼
┌─────────────────────────────────────────────────────┐
│ EFMP will appear on Soldiers ERB                    │
└─────────────────────────────────────────────────────┘
```

REFERENCES:
AR 608-75

Health and Welfare Inspections

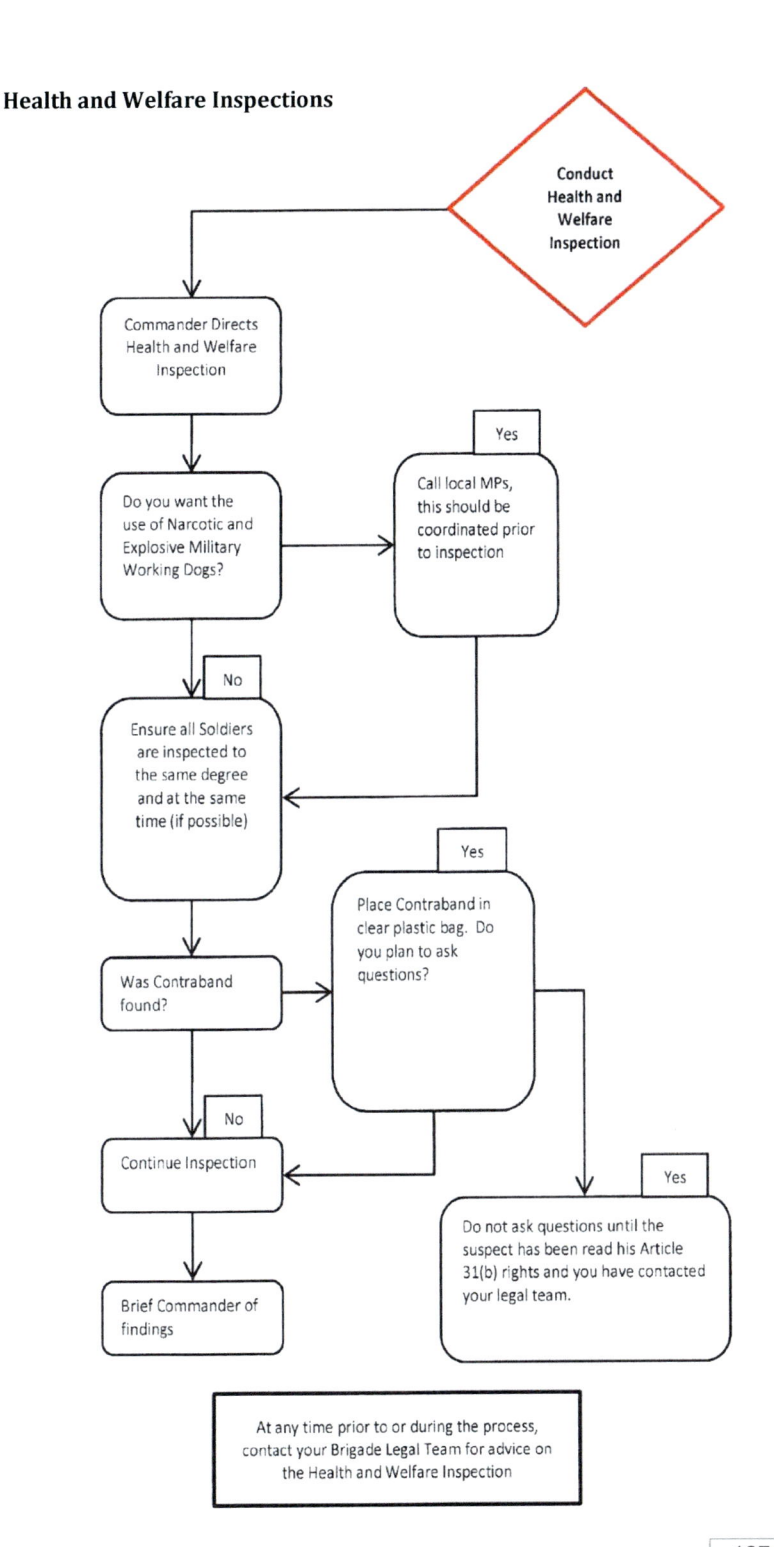

Conduct Health and Welfare Inspection

- Commander Directs Health and Welfare Inspection
- Do you want the use of Narcotic and Explosive Military Working Dogs?
  - **Yes** → Call local MPs, this should be coordinated prior to inspection
  - **No** → Ensure all Soldiers are inspected to the same degree and at the same time (if possible)
- Was Contraband found?
  - **Yes** → Place Contraband in clear plastic bag. Do you plan to ask questions?
    - **Yes** → Do not ask questions until the suspect has been read his Article 31(b) rights and you have contacted your legal team.
  - **No** → Continue Inspection
- Brief Commander of findings

At any time prior to or during the process, contact your Brigade Legal Team for advice on the Health and Welfare Inspection

FLOW CHARTS

Off Post Apprehension / Confinement

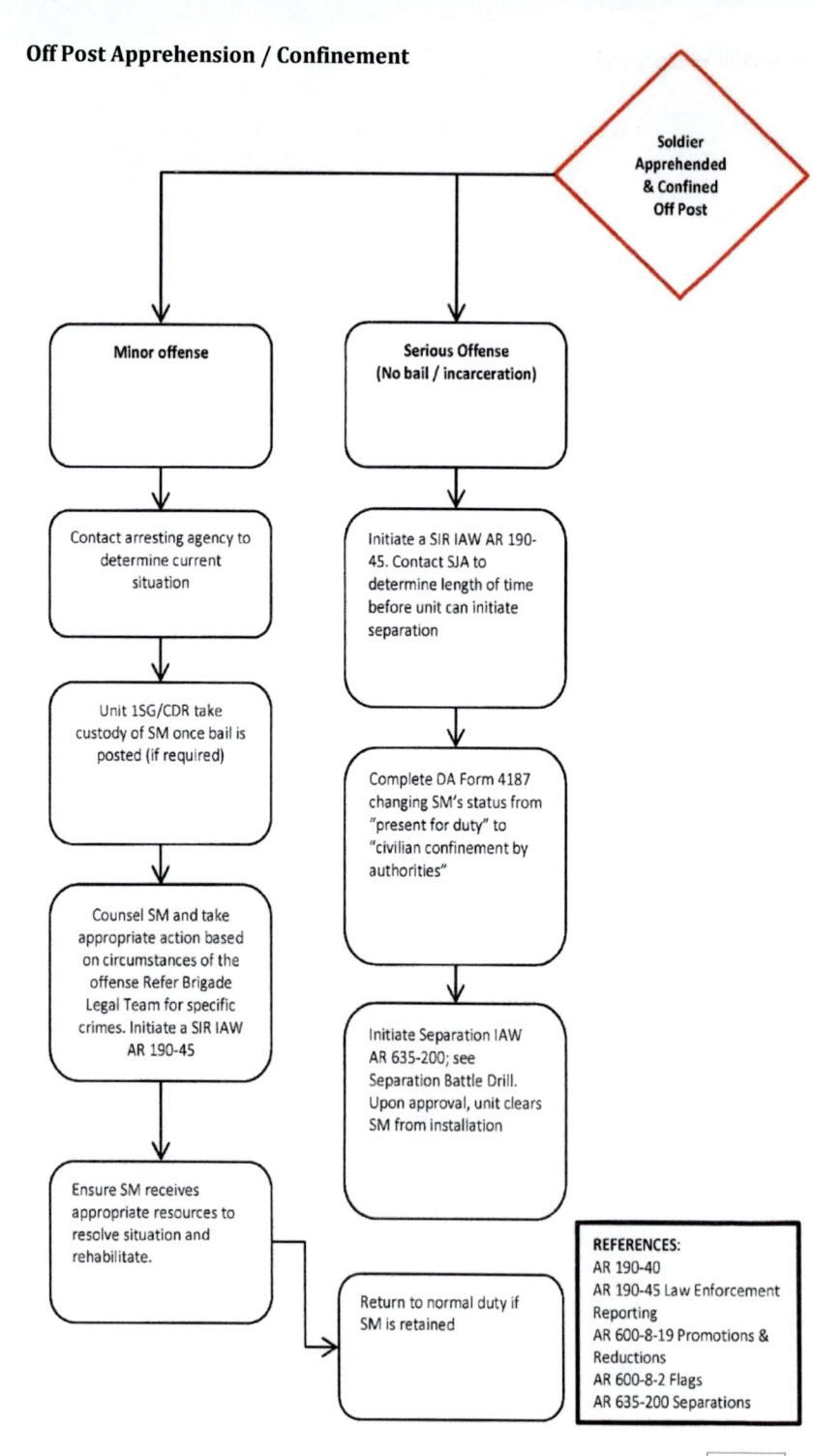

Soldier Apprehended & Confined Off Post

Minor offense

- Contact arresting agency to determine current situation
- Unit 1SG/CDR take custody of SM once bail is posted (if required)
- Counsel SM and take appropriate action based on circumstances of the offense Refer Brigade Legal Team for specific crimes. Initiate a SIR IAW AR 190-45
- Ensure SM receives appropriate resources to resolve situation and rehabilitate.

Serious Offense (No bail / incarceration)

- Initiate a SIR IAW AR 190-45. Contact SJA to determine length of time before unit can initiate separation
- Complete DA Form 4187 changing SM's status from "present for duty" to "civilian confinement by authorities"
- Initiate Separation IAW AR 635-200; see Separation Battle Drill. Upon approval, unit clears SM from installation

Return to normal duty if SM is retained

REFERENCES:
AR 190-40
AR 190-45 Law Enforcement Reporting
AR 600-8-19 Promotions & Reductions
AR 600-8-2 Flags
AR 635-200 Separations

Advancement Wavers

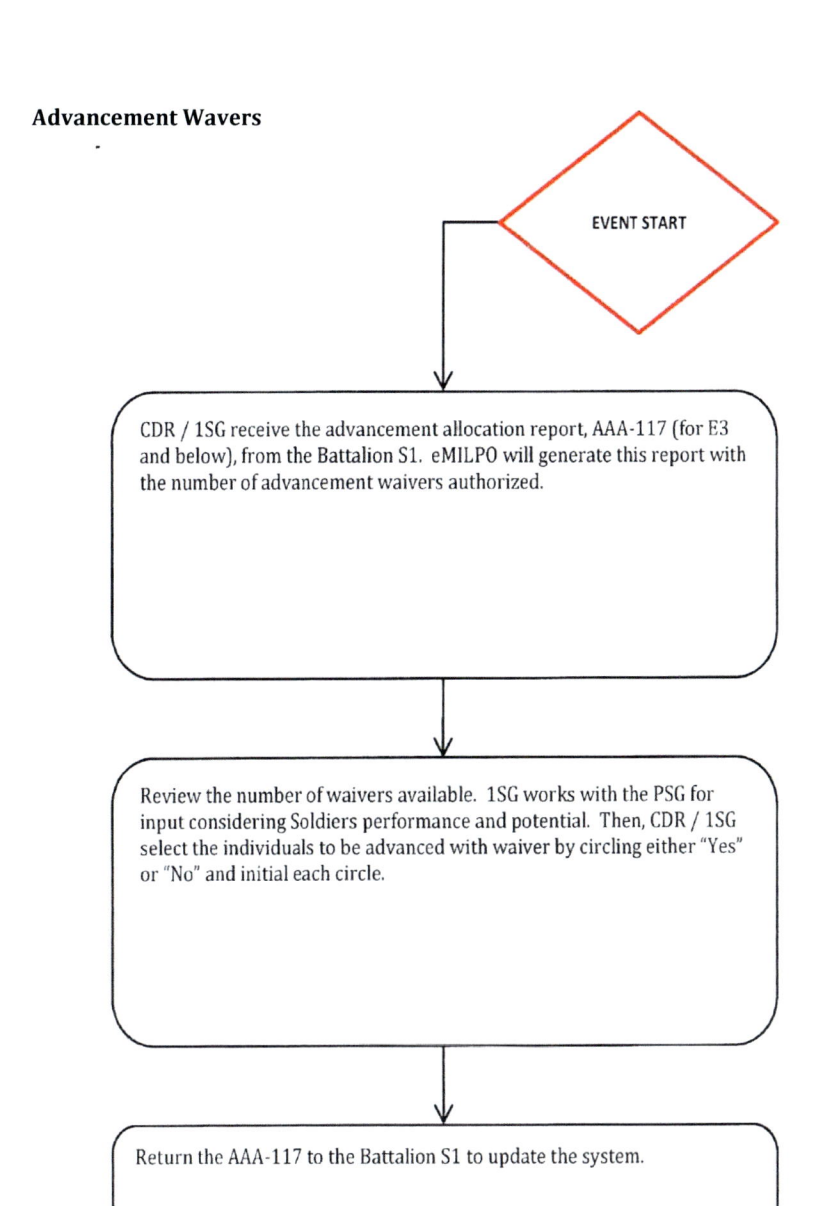

```
EVENT START
```

CDR / 1SG receive the advancement allocation report, AAA-117 (for E3 and below), from the Battalion S1. eMILPO will generate this report with the number of advancement waivers authorized.

Review the number of waivers available. 1SG works with the PSG for input considering Soldiers performance and potential. Then, CDR / 1SG select the individuals to be advanced with waiver by circling either "Yes" or "No" and initial each circle.

Return the AAA-117 to the Battalion S1 to update the system.

REFERENCES:
AR 600-8-19
AAA-117

Reference Information

Reference Manuals

NCO CREED	TC 22-6
CBRN	FM 3-11
FIRST AID	FM 4-25.11
PHYSICAL TRAINING	FM 7-22
MAP READING-LAND NAVIGATION	FM 3-25.26
MILITARY LEADERSHIP	FM 6-22 / ADRP 6-22
SOLDIER TEAM DEVELOPMENT	FM 22-102
DRILL AND CEREMONIES	FM 3-21.5
GUARD DUTY	FM 22-6
INDIVIDUAL WEAPONS	FM 3-22.31 / 3-22.9
TRAINING THE FORCE	FM 7-0
BATTLE FOCUS TRAINING	FM 7-1
LEGAL GUIDE FOR CDRS	FM 27-1
THE ARMY PROFESSION	ADRP 1
TERMS AND MILITARY SYMBOLS	ADRP 1-02
INTELLIGENCE	ADRP 2-0
UNIFIED LAND OPERATIONS	ADRP 3-0
SUSTAINMENT	ADRP 4-0
THE OPERATIONS PROCESS	ADRP 5-0
MISSION COMMAND	ADRP 6-0
ARMY LEADERSHIP	ADRP 6-22
TRAINING UNITS AND DEVELOPING LDRS	ADRP 7-0
UCMJ	AR 27-10
CODE OF CONDUCT	AR 350-30
NCO PROFESSIONAL DEVELOP.	AR 350-17
IND. MIL. EDUCATION & TNG	AR 351-1
CORRESPONDENCE PROGRAM	AR 351-20
THE ARMY SAFETY PROGRAM	AR 385-10
WEIGHT CONTROL	AR 600-9
COMMAND POLICY	AR 600-20
EQUAL OPPORTUNITY	AR 600-20
CUSTOMS AND COURTESIES	AR 600-25
ENLISTED PERS. MANAGEMENT	AR 600-200
UNFAVORABLE ACTION INFO	AR 600-37
STANDARDS OF CONDUCT	AR 600-50
SEL. FOR TNG & ASSIGNMENT	AR 614-200
CONTINUING EDUCATION	AR 621-5
ENLISTED EVAL REP SYSTEM	AR 623-3
INDIVIDUAL PERSONNEL SYSTEM	AR 640-10
PHOTO'S FOR PERSONNEL	AR 640-30
WEAR OF THE UNIFORM	AR 670-1
MILITARY AWARDS	AR 672-5-1
MILITARY PERSONNEL ORG.	AR 680-29
ENLISTED CAREER MANAGEMENT	DA CIR 611-82-3
NCO EVAL. REPORTING SYSTEM	DA CIR 623-88-1
NCOER SYSTEM "IN BRIEF"	DA PAM 623-205
MIL. PERSONNEL MANAGEMENT	DA PAM 600-8
USAREUR TRAINING DIRECTIVE	USAREUR R350-1

MIRANDA RIGHTS WARNING STATEMENT

VERBAL RIGHTS WARNING
Inform the person of your official position, the nature of the offense(s), and the fact that he/she is suspect/accused. Then read him/her the following – do not paraphrase; read verbatim:

`BEFORE I ASK YOU ANY QUESTIONS, YOU MUST UNDERSTAND YOUR RIGHT.´
1. You do not have to answer my questions or say anything.
2. Anything you say or do can be used as evidence against you in a criminal trial.
3. **(For personnel subject to the UCMJ)** you have the right to talk privately to a lawyer before, during, and after Questioning and to have a lawyer present with you during questioning. This lawyer can be a civilian you arrange for at no expense to the government or a military Lawyer detailed for you at no expense to you or both.
4. **(For civilian not subject to the UCMJ)** you have the right to talk privately to a lawyer before, during, and after Questioning and to have a lawyer present with you during questioning. This lawyer can be one you arrange for at your own expense, or if you cannot afford a lawyer and want one, a lawyer will be appointed for you before any questioning begins.
5. If you are now willing to discuss the offense(s) under Investigation, with or without a lawyer present, you have A right to stop answering questions at any time, or speak Privately with a lawyer before answering further, even if
6. You sign a waiver certificate.

Make certain the suspect/accused fully understands his/her rights.
Then say:

DO YOU WANT A LAWYER AT THIS TIME?

AT THIS TIME, ARE YOU WILLING TO DISCUSS THE OFFENSE(S) UNDER INVESTIGATION AND MAKE A STATEMENT WITHOUT TALKING TO A LAWYER AND WITHOUT HAVING A LAWYER PRESENT WITH YOU?

Punitive articles UCMJ

Article 77- Principals
Article 78-Accessory after the fact
Article 79-Conviction of lesser-included offenses
Article 80-Attempts
Article 81-Conspiracy
Article 82-Solicitation
Article 83-Fraudulent enlistment, appointment, or separation
Article 84-Effecting unlawful enlistment, appointment, or separation
Article 85-Desertion
Article 86-Absence without leave
Article 87-Missing movement
Article 88-Contempt toward officials
Article 89-Disrespect toward a superior commissioned officer
Article 90-Assaulting or willfully disobeying superior commissioned officer
Article 91-Insubordinate conduct toward warrant officer, noncommissioned officer, or petty officer
Article 92-Failure to obey order or regulation
Article 93-Cruelty and maltreatment
Article 94-Mutiny and sedation
Article 95-Resistance, Flight, breach of arrest, and escape
Article 96-Releasing prisoner without proper authority
Article 97-Unlawful detention
Article 98-Noncompliance with procedural rules
Article 99-Misbehavior before the enemy
Article 100-Subordinate compelling surrender
Article 101-Improper use of countersign
Article 102-Forcing a safeguard
Article 103-Captured or abandoned property
Article 104-Aiding the enemy
Article 105-Misconduct as a prisoner
Article 106-Spies
Article 106a-Espionage
Article 107-False official statements
Article 108-Military property of the United States-sale, loss, damage, destruction, or wrongful disposition
Article 109-Property other than military property of the United States-waste, spoilage, or destruction
Article 110-Improper hazarding of vessel
Article 111-Drunken or reckless operation of vehicle, aircraft, or vessel
Article 112-Drunk on duty
Article 112a-Wrongful use, possession, etc., of controlled substances
Article 113-Misbehaving of sentinel or lookout
Article 114-Dueling
Article 115-Malingering
Article 116-Riot or breach of peace
Article 117-Provoking speeches or gestures

Article 118-Murder
Article 119-Manslaughter
Article 120-Rape and carnal knowledge
Article 121-Larceny and wrongful appropriation
Article 122-Robbery
Article 123-Forgery
Article 123a-Making, Drawing, or uttering check, draft, or order without sufficient funds
Article 124-Maiming
Article 125-Sodomy
Article 126-Arson
Article 127-Extortion
Article 128-Assault
Article 129-Buglary
Article 130-Housbreaking
Article 131-Perjury
Article 132-Frauds against the United States
Article 133-Conduct unbecoming an officer and gentleman

Article 134-General article

Paragraph 61 -(Abusing public animal)
Paragraph 62 -(Adultery)
Paragraph 63 -(Assault-incident)
Paragraph 64 -(Assault-with intent to commit murder, voluntary manslaughter, rape, robbery, sodomy, arson, burglary, or housebreaking)
Paragraph 65 -(Bigamy)
Paragraph 66 -(Bribery and graft)
Paragraph 67 -(Burning with intent to defraud)
Paragraph 68 -(Check, worthless, making and uttering-by dishonorably failing to maintain funds)
Paragraph 69 -(Cohabitation, wrongful)
Paragraph 70 -(Correctional custody-offenses against)
Paragraph 71 -(Debt, dishonorably failing to pay)
Paragraph 72 -(Disloyal statements)
Paragraph 73 -(Disorderly conduct, drunkenness)
Paragraph 74 -(Drinking liquor with prisoner)
Paragraph 75 -(Drunk prisoner)
Paragraph 76 -(Drunkenness-incapacitation for performance of duties through prior wrongful indulgence in intoxicating liquor or any drug)
Paragraph 77 -(False or unauthorized pass offenses)
Paragraph 78 –(False pretenses, obtaining services under)
Paragraph 79 – (False swearing)
Paragraph 80 –(Firearm, discharging – through negligence)
Paragraph 81 – (Firearm, discharging – willfully, under such circumstances as to endanger human life)
Paragraph 82 – (Fleeing scene of accident)
Paragraph 83 – (Fraternization)

Paragraph 84 – (Gambling with subordinate)
Paragraph 85 – (Homicide, negligent)
Paragraph 86 – (Impersonating a commissioned, warrant, noncommissioned, or petty officer, or an agent of official)
Paragraph 87 – (Indecent acts of liberties with a child)
Paragraph 88 – (Indecent exposure)
Paragraph 89 – (Indecent language)
Paragraph 90 – (Indecent acts with another)
Paragraph 91 – (Jumping from vessel into the water)
Paragraph 92 – (Kidnapping)
Paragraph 93 – (Mail: taking, opening, secreting, destroying, or stealing)
Paragraph 94 – (Mails: depositing or causing to be deposited obscene matters in)
Paragraph 95 – (Misprison of serious offense)
Paragraph 96 – (Obstructing justice)
Paragraph 97 – (Pandering and prostitution)
Paragraph 98 – (Perjury: subornation of)Paragraph 99 – (Public record: altering, concealing, removing, mutilating, obliterating, or destroying)
Paragraph 100 – (Quarantine: medicle, breaking)
Paragraph 101 – (Requesting commission of an offence)
Paragraph 102 – (Restriction, breaking)
Paragraph 103 – (Seizure: destruction, removal, or disposal of property to prevent)
Paragraph 104 – (Sentinel or lookout: offences against or by)
Paragraph 105 – (Soliciting another to commit an offense)
Paragraph 106 – (Stolen property: knowingly receiving, buying, concealing)
Paragraph 107 – (Straggling)
Paragraph 108 – (Testify: wrongful refusal)
Paragraph 109 – (Threat or hoax: bomb)
Paragraph 110 – (Threat, communicating)
Paragraph 111 – (Unlawful entry)
Paragraph 112 – (Weapon: concealed, carrying)
Paragraph 113 – (Wearing unauthorized insignia, decoration, badge, ribbon, device, or lapel button)

Acronyms

A

ACR Advanced Concepts and Requirements

ACR/RDA Advanced Concepts And Requirements/ Research, Development and Acquisition

ACTD Advanced Concepts and Technology Demonstration

ACV OPFOR Armored Command Vehicle

AD Air Defense

ADST Advanced Distributed Simulation Technology

ADST II Advanced Distributed Simulation Technology II

AGL Automatic Grenade Launcher

AGM Air-Ground Missile

AIDS Acquired Immune Deficiency Syndrome

AIM Advanced Integrated Management

AMEL Active Matrix Electro-Luminescence

AMSO Army Model and Simulation Office

AP Anti-Personnel

AP/AT Anti-Personnel/Anti-Tank

APC Armored Personnel Carrier

APDS-T Armor Piercing Discarding Sabot - Tracer

APFSDS-T Armor Piercing Fin Stabilized Discarding Sabot - Tracer

API Armor Piercing Incendiary

API-T Armor Piercing Incendiary - Tracer

ARI Army Research Institute

ARPA Advanced Research Projects Agency

ARTEP U.S. Army Training and Evaluation Program

ARTEP-MTP U.S. Army Training and Evaluation Program-Mission Training Plans

AT Antitank

ATD Advanced Technology Demonstration

ATGL Antitank Grenade Launcher

ATGM Antitank Guided Missile

AUD Audible

AUSA Association of the U.S. Army

AVLB Armored Vehicle Launch Bridge

AWE Army Warfighting Experiment

B

BCS Battery Computer System

BFV Bradley Fighting Vehicle

BLEP Ballistic Eye Protection

BLUFOR Other Friendly Forces

BMP OPFOR Amphibious Infantry Combat Vehicle

BN Battalion

BOS Battlefield Operating System

BRDM OPFOR Amphibious Scout/Reconnaissance Vehicle

BTR OPFOR Amphibious Armored Personnel Carrier

BUCS Back-up Computer System

C

C2 Command and Control

C4I Command, Control, Communications, Computers and Intelligence

CAS Close Air Support

CATT Combined Arms Tactical Trainer

CB Chemical and Biological

CCO Close Combat Optic

CCOS Close Combat Optic Sight

CCTT Close Combat Tactical Trainer

CDRL Contract Data Requirements List

CFE Contractor Furnished Equipment
CGF Computer Generated Forces
CIS Combat Instruction Sets
CITV Commander's Independent Thermal Viewer
CO Company / Commanding Officer
COEA Cost and Operational Effectiveness Analysis
COMSEC Communications Security
CPX Command Post Exercise
CRS Computer/Radio Subsystem
CTA Clothing Table of Allowance
C/VAM Compass/Vertical Angle Measurement
CW Clockwise

D
DBBL Dismounted Battlespace Battle Lab
DCIM Display Control Interface Module
DDC Day Display Component
DI Dismounted Infantry
DIS Distributed Interactive Simulation
DoD Department of Defense
DP Developmental Priority
DPICM Dual-Purpose Improved Conventional Munitions
DSSU Dismounted Soldier System Unit
DTO Digital Terminal Operator
DWN Dismounted Infantry Warrior Network

E
EMA External Mount Assembly
EOE Early Operational Experimentation
EPW Enemy Prisoners of War

F
FA Field Artillery
FAV Fast Attack Vehicle
FBCB2 Force XXI Battle Command Brigade and Below

FD Fire Direction
FDP Functional Definition Process
FLIR Forward Looking Infrared
FM Field Manuals
FO Forward Observer
FOV Field of View
FPC Functional Process Code
FROG OPFOR Free Rocket Over Ground
FSO Fire Support Officer
FSRC Foreign Systems Research Center
FTX Field Training Exercise
FWA Fixed Wing Aircraft
FY Fiscal Year

G
GAC Ground Assault Convoy
GCP Ground Commander's Pointer
GEN II Generation II
GFE Government Furnished Equipment
GFI Government Furnished Information
GPS Global Positioning System
GRAYFOR Gray Forces

H
H&W Health and Welfare
HE High Explosive
HEAT High Explosive Antitank
HEAT-FS High-Explosive Antitank - Fin Stabilized
HEAT-MP-T High-Explosive Antitank - Multipurpose - Tracer
HEI High-Explosive Incendiary
HEMTT Heavy Expanded Mobility Tactical Truck
HESH High-Explosive Squash Head
HHC Headquarters and Headquarters Company

HHD Handheld Display

HMD Head-Mounted Monocular Display

HMG Heavy Machine Gun

HMMWV High Mobility Multipurpose Wheeled Vehicle

HQ Headquarters

HVAPFSDS Hyper-Velocity Armor Piercing Fin Stabilized Discarding Sabot

I

I2 Image Intensification

IC Individual Combatant

ICM Improved Conventional Munitions

ID Identification

IFV Infantry Fighting Vehicle

IEDK Individual Equipment Decontamination Kit

IHAS Integrated Helmet Assembly Subsystem

IR Infrared

ISU Integrated Sight Unit

ITS(s) Individual Training Standards

IUSS Integrated Unit Simulation System

L

LANTIRN Low Altitude Navigation Targeting Infrared Night

LAW Light Antitank Weapon

LCE Load Carrying Equipment

LCMS Laser Countermeasures System
LED Light-Emitting Diode

LIF Laser Interference Filter

LMG Light Machine Gun

LMTV Light Medium Tactical Vehicle

LOS Line of Sight

LRF/DC Laser Range Finder/Digital Compass

LTA Launch Tube Assembly

LW Land Warrior

LWTB Land Warrior Test Bed

M

M & S Modeling And Simulation

MBST Marine Battle Skills Training

MC&G Mapping, Charting, and Geodesy

MCCDC Marine Corps Combat Development Command

MCCRES USMC Combat Readiness Evaluation

MEDEVAC Medical Evacuation

MELIOS Mini-Eyesafe Laser Infrared Observation Set

METT-T Mission, Enemy, Terrain, Troops, And Time Available

MG Machine Gun

MLRF MELIOS Laser Rangefinder

MM millimeter

MNS Mission Need Statement

MOBA Military Operations In Built-Up Area

ModSAF Modular Semi-Automated Forces

MOPP Mission-Oriented Protective Posture

MOS Military Occupational Specialty

MOUT Military Operations on Urbanized Terrain

MTOE Modified Table of Organization and Equipment

MTP Mission Training Plans

MTV Medium Tactical Vehicle

MW Modular Weapon

MWS Modular Weapon System

N

NA Not Applicable

NATO North Atlantic Treaty Organization

NAV Navigation

NBC Nuclear, Biological, Chemical

NCO Noncommissioned Officer

NDC Night Display Component

NIMA National Imagery and Mapping Agency's

N-LOS Non-Line of Sight

NODL Night Observation Device, Long Range

NSDC Night Sensor/Display Component

NUM Numeric

NVD Night Vision Device

NVG Night Vision Goggles

O

OCCFLD Occupational Field

OICW Objective Integrated Individual Combat Weapon

OLG Objective Lens Group

OOTW Operations Other Than War

OP Observation Post

OPFOR Opposing Forces

ORD Operational Requirements Document

OT Operator Tasks

P

PC Personal Computer

PCIES Protective Clothing and Individual Equipment Subsystem

PEWS Platoon Early Warning System

PL Platoon Leader

PLGR Precision Lightweight Global Positioning System Receiver

PLT Platoon

PM-CATT Project Manager for Combined Arms Tactical Trainer

PNVS Pilot's Night Vision Sensor

POI Program of Instruction

POL Petroleum, Oils, Lubricants

POS Position

PPS Pulse-Per-Second

PSG Platoon Sergeant

PSM Personnel System Monitor

PTL Primary Task List

PTT Push-To-Talk

PUA Primary Using Audience

R

R&D Research and Development

RAP Rocket-Assisted Projectile

RCI Resource Consultants Incorporated

RDA Research, Development And Acquisition

RDF Rapid Disruption Force

RDFD Requirement Decomposition Functional Definition

RF Radio Frequency

RFL Restricted Fire Line

RIPD Remote Input/Pointing Device

RIS Rail Interface System

RL Rocket Launcher

RPG Rocket Propelled Grenade

RSM Regimental Sergeant Major

RT Radio Transmitter

RTO Radio Telephone Operator

RWA Rotary Wing Aircraft

S

SAF Semi-Automated Forces

SAIC Science Application International Corporation

SAM Surface-to-Air Missile

SASO Stability and Security Operations

SAW Squad Automatic Weapon

SI Situational Interrupt

SIMNET Simulation Network

SINCGARS Single Channel Ground and Airborne Radio System

SITREP Situation Report

SLP Semi active Laser-Guided Projectile

SMCT Soldier's Manual of Common Tasks

SME Subject Matter Experts

SMMP System Manprint Master Plan

SNS Sniper Night Scope

SOP Standard Operating Procedure

SPF Special Purpose Force

SPKR/MIC Speaker/Microphone

SQD Squad

SQDN Squadron

SSD Structured Self Development

SSM Surface-to-Surface Missile

ST Special Text

STs Special Texts

STOW Synthetic Theater of War

STP Soldier Training Publication

STRADIS Simulation and Training Aid for the Dismounted Soldier

STRICOM Simulation, Training And Instrumentation Command

T

T&E Test And Evaluation

T/E Tables of Equipment

T/O Table of Organization

TACFIRE Tactical Fire Direction System

TADS Target Acquisition and Designation System

TAS Target Acquisition System

TBESC Technology Base Executive Steering Committee

TDR Training Device Requirement

TEISS-D The Enhanced Integrated Soldier System-Dismounted

TEMO Training Exercise and Military Operations

TEWG Technical Executive Working Group

TIC Technology Insertion Candidate

TM Technical Manual

TOE Table of Equipment

TO&E Tables of Organization and Equipment

TOW Tube-Launched, Optically-Tracked, Wire-Guided

TRP Target Reference Points

TPSC Task Performance Support Code

TRADOC U.S. Army Training and Doctrine Command

TRAC-WSMR TRADOC Analysis Center, White Sands Missile Range

TWS Thermal Weapon Sight

U

UCMJ Uniform Code of Military Justice

USAF U.S. Air Force

USAICS U.S. Army Infantry Center and School

USAIS U.S. Army Infantry School

USMC United States Marine Corps

UXO Unexploded Ordnance

V

VAM Vertical Angle Measurement

VDC Volts Direct Current

VIS Visual

VV&A Verification, Validation and Accreditation

W

WP White Phosphorus

WS Weapon Subsystem

WSS Weapon Subsystem

X

XO Executive Officer

Z

ZU OPFOR Antiaircraft Gun

ZPU OPFOR Antiaircraft Gun

ZSU OPFOR Self Propelled Antiaircraft Vehicle

About the Author

BIOGRAPHY

First Sergeant **Jessie W. Sasser**

First Sergeant Jessie W. Sasser entered the United States Army on 21 March 1995 from Orange, TX. Graduated Honor Soldier from Basic Training and AIT at Ft. Knox, KY as a 63T Bradley Fighting Vehicle Mechanic.

1SG Sasser was assigned to 2-8th Infantry, 2nd Brigade, 4th Infantry Division Ft. Hood, TX as a mechanic and recovery specialist. While assigned to 2-8 Infantry he won 2nd Brigade Soldier of the Quarter and 4th Infantry Division Mechanic of the Quarter 1997. He also received several commendations for service and support during this time. He was then assigned to 1-6th Infantry, 2nd Brigade, 1st Armored Division Baumholder, Germany as a maintenance team squad leader. 1SG Sasser won 2nd Brigade Soldier of the Quarter, 2nd Brigade NCO of the Year, Honor Graduate from WLC and deployed to Kosovo with TF Falcon 1999 to 2000. Upon completion of his tour in Kosovo, he was assigned to B FSC, 215th FSB, 1st Cavalry Division, Ft. Hood, TX. There he served as a Maintenance Platoon Sergeant. In 2003, 1SG Sasser was selected for 1st Special Forces US ARMY SPECIAL OPERATIONS COMMAND. In December 2009 1SG Sasser was assigned to HHC 1st BCT, 82nd Airborne Division, Ft. Bragg, NC. He deployed to Iraq 09-10 with the Brigade Staff in support of Operation Iraqi Freedom. After returning from deployment he assumed First Sergeant for Delta Troop 3-73 CAV, 1st BCT. 1SG Sasser deployed to Afghanistan in March 2012 in support of Operation Enduring Freedom.

1SG Sasser's military education includes WLC, ALC, SLC, Pre Command Course, Master Fitness Trainers Course, Airborne School, Jumpmaster Course, Military Free Fall Parachutist Course (HALO), SERE School level 1,2,and 3, Welding School, Defensive and Offensive Driving, Automotive Acquisition Course, Combat Support Course; Combatives Course Level I and II and the Combat Life Savers Course.

His awards and decorations include the Bronze Star Medal (2OLC); Meritorious Service Medal (1OLC); Joint Service Commendation Medal (1OLC); Army Commendation Medal (3OLC); Army Achievement Medal (5OLC); National Defense Service Medal (1OLC); Army Good Conduct Medal (6th Award); Kosovo Campaign Medal (BSS); Global War On Terrorism Expeditionary Medal; Global War On Terrorism Service Medal; Iraqi Campaign Medal (2CSS); Afghanistan Campaign Medal (CSS); Overseas Service Ribbon; Army Service Ribbon; NCO Professional Development Ribbon (Numeral 3); NATO Medal; NATO Kosovo; NATO ISAF; Combat Action Badge; Parachutist Badge; Military Free Fall Badge; Mechanic Badge; Drivers Badge Wheel/Track. German Airborne Badge (Bronze); Canadian Airborne Badge (Red); and the Australian Airborne Badge. 1SG Sasser is also a Samuel Sharp Award Recipient.

Made in the USA
Columbia, SC
21 November 2018